How to Capitalize on the Video Revolution

How to Capitalize on the Video Revolution

A Guide to New Business Enterprises

Charlene Canape

Holt, Rinehart and Winston
New York

Copyright © 1984 by Charlene Canape
All rights reserved, including the right to reproduce this
book or portions thereof in any form.
Published by Holt, Rinehart and Winston,
383 Madison Avenue, New York, New York 10017.
Published simultaneously in Canada by Holt, Rinehart
and Winston of Canada, Limited.

Library of Congress Cataloging in Publication Data
Canape, Charlene.
How to capitalize on the video revolution.
Includes index.
1. Video tape industry.   2. New business enterprises.
3. Entrepreneur.   I. Title.
HD9697.V542C36   1984   621.388'332   83-26534
ISBN: 0-03-070343-3

First Edition

Designer: Joy Taylor
Printed in the United States of America
1 3 5 7 9 10 8 6 4 2

ISBN 0-03-070343-3

To my two guys, Tom and Joseph

Contents

Acknowledgments

THE SEED for this book was planted several years ago while I was working as media and advertising editor for *Business Week*. Because of my contacts in the broadcast and cable television industries, many entrepreneurs sought my advice on starting video businesses. After I left *Business Week* to freelance, I still encountered many people who were seeking information on video. I finally decided there was a need for a book that could assist these people.

During my reporting, I met many video entrepreneurs. Some were very successful, others were still struggling. All of them were very generous with their time and were willing to share their experiences and expertise. I owe each one a great debt. Their observations and thoughtful comments added immeasurably to this work.

I am also grateful to the many experts whose insights served to clarify the issues confronting those working in video. These valuable sources include Peter Diamandis, Jim Perkins, Tony Hoffman, Henry Kaplan, Barbara Dill, Al Hampel, Greg Blaine, Dave Simons, Gregory Joseph, Joe Ostrow, and Ray McArdle.

I would like to thank my editor at Holt, Rinehart and

Winston, Bobbi Mark, and my agent, Denise Marcil. Each offered the encouragement and guidance I needed to see this project through to completion. A special thanks to my dear friend Bonnie Siverd, whose advice, based on her own book-writing experiences, I found invaluable.

My deepest gratitude to Cathy Joseph, whose expert care of my infant son enabled me to complete the book on schedule. And, most of all, to my parents and mother-in-law, whose love, support, and interest in my work have been a source of inspiration for me.

Finally, to my husband, Tom, and son, Joseph, who together have provided me with a most loving home from which to create.

How to Capitalize on the Video Revolution

Introduction

In the 1950s, when Americans gathered in front of their black and white television sets to watch "The Texaco Star Theater," with emcee Milton Berle, they never dreamed of all that the black box would be used for by the 1980s. It was incredible enough that they could turn a knob and actually watch events taking place in a studio far away. Who could have envisioned a video revolution that would bring to the market videocassettes, videodisks, video games, large-screen TV, and interactive services that allow someone to shop, bank, or vote from home?

The television, once considered a luxury, is now a necessity. According to A.C. Nielsen, there are now more than 80 million homes with television in the United States, and that number continues to grow each year. In fact, the typical American family has TV sets scattered throughout the house in order to provide each member freedom of choice.

While the consumer initially may have bought his TV set to watch Monday night football or the evening news, now that it is in his home he is discovering that it is the key to a lot more. The three major TV networks no longer monopolize the viewer's time. Cable and pay-TV provide him with other programming choices.

More dramatic change is occurring. The videocassette recorder (VCR) has given the consumer more control over what he watches—and when he watches it. By hooking up a VCR to his television, the consumer can record a program for later viewing or record one program while he is watching another. He can even enjoy a recent movie by renting a prerecorded videocassette. He merely pops the cassette into his VCR and, voilà! a movie theater in his living room.

The video revolution was made possible by videotape, a magnetic tape coated with iron oxide that is capable of recording both images and sounds for future playback. Videotape was first perfected for professional use back in the mid-sixties, and it quickly gained in popularity because it holds so many attractions for the television industry.

Unlike film, videotape does not have to be processed, thus making possible instant sports replays and the immediate coverage of news events. Videotape also is cheaper than film, and is used by the three major networks for recording daytime soap operas, which have smaller budgets than prime-time programming.

Despite its many advantages, videotape will never replace film for prime-time television shows and theatrical movies. The reason? Videotape cannot deliver the high-quality images that film can. With film, lighting can be used to achieve soft shadows, adding texture and depth to each scene. With videotape, lighting often produces glare and neon colors. Even though videotape will improve as technology advances, film will still be superior in quality. In addition, videotape, because it is magnetic, does not last as long as film. So it is difficult to imagine Hollywood's directors forgoing film's artistic elements or longer life to save time or money with video.

Indeed, when a consumer watches a major motion picture on a big screen in a movie theater, he is able to appreciate fully the aesthetic qualities of film. But seated in his living room, before his five-year-old TV, such qualities are less important to him. He is accustomed to seeing videotape used in sports, news, daytime programs, and even some popular situation comedies like "All in the Family."

In the late 1970s, after the consumer had adjusted to the look of videotape, Sony introduced the videocassette recorder. There were many eager buyers for the Sony Betamax, as the system is still called, particularly because it had many convenient features for the consumer. First of all, the videotape was packaged in a cassette. Sony earlier had marketed an open-reel video system, but many consumers found the system difficult to operate. A videocassette made everything much simpler.

Sony's Betamax included other enticements. A timer enabled the consumer to videotape a television program or movie while he was out. He also could record one program while watching another. Soon, companies began to sell and rent movies on videocassettes, allowing consumers to use their VCRs to watch big-screen hits on their TV sets. Home entertainment would never be the same.

It is estimated that in 1976, Sony sold 30,000 Betamax units. By 1977, that figure had grown to 200,000. Other manufacturers entered the market in 1978, and sales reached more than 400,000. Today about 10 percent of American homes have one or more VCRs, for a total of more than 7 million, and that number is expected to increase every year.

By 1979, the video equipment manufacturers were marketing video cameras for use in the home. With a VCR and a video camera, the consumer could fashion his own TV entertainment—shooting his own productions and watching them on his TV screen.

Even the most unlikely candidates found themselves hooked on the new video technology. That phenomenon continues. The person who may never have thought about buying a home movie camera cannot resist the lure of home video. For one thing, home video is more convenient and less intimidating than many of those old home movie systems. (Remember rewinding those reels and setting up the projection screen?) And the prices for many video products have been declining, bringing video systems within reach of the average American family.

Once the consumer has invested money in a VCR and a video camera, he looks for other ways to put his video equipment to good use. He may never have imagined having his daughter's wedding videotaped, but now that he owns a VCR and can watch the tape anytime, the idea makes sense.

Because he is more familiar with video, he is receptive to many new uses he may not have considered before. If he is single and looking to meet someone new, joining a video dating service does not seem so strange to him.

He begins to find uses for video that could improve his work life, too. If he is a lawyer, he may think about using video to take a witness's deposition or to record a client's will. The corporate executive begins to explore video's usefulness in communicating with his employees. The job candidate considers making a video résumé to impress prospective employers. Aspiring musicians use videotapes of their performances for auditions.

Each new application for video creates business opportunities. This book is filled with examples of entrepreneurs who started with an idea and saw it through to create a video business. Are these people technology freaks? Visionaries? Some yes, some no. But they all have something in common. They identified what they perceived to be a real need for a new service or product. And they saw video as fulfilling that need.

Not all of these businesses will make it. It is a well-known fact that new businesses are vulnerable to failure, and surely video businesses are not immune. Have no illusions. The appeal of video alone is not enough to keep a struggling business afloat.

But many of these businesses have already succeeded. (Some of the video dating services have even begun selling franchises.) Others will succeed, too.

The goal of this book is to stimulate your own thinking about video. You will receive some guidelines to help you determine whether video is the field for you. You will be given information on how to develop, evaluate, and sell your video idea. You will learn about setting up, protecting, and equipping your business. And you will meet some of the successful video professionals who are selling their services to entertainers, lawyers, corporations, and consumers.

By the end, you will have enough information to formulate your own game plan. The video revolution has begun and shows no signs of dying down. Are you one of the people who will find its lure irresistible?

1

Is the Video Revolution for Me?

MANY PEOPLE are intimidated by video. That reaction is understandable. Video promises to change the way we live, work, and play. For many, change can be unsettling. There is the urge to protect the status quo, to continue to do things the way they have been done for years and years.

The passage of time will no doubt make acceptance easier for most people. In fact, all pioneering inventions were once greeted with skepticism. Jim Perkins, who launched many cable projects, including "The Home Shopping Show" in Chicago, said: "Everyone's confrontation with new technology comes in different stages. I can remember, when I was a kid, people saying they weren't sure they needed a telephone. Others took time to adjust to motion pictures."

Of course, the younger generation is having less trouble adjusting, as anyone who has ventured near a video game arcade recently can attest. "The kids are already into it," said Jim Perkins. "These kids with their joy sticks are TV kids. They were brought up on it. The older generation is moving boldly forward into the future with both feet firmly planted in the past."

There are, however, adults who are enthusiastic about video. These are the entrepreneurs who are launching video businesses. Interviews with numerous video entrepreneurs make one thing obvious: no two are alike. All seem to have come to the field via different routes. For some, that route was direct, for others, circuitous. Several of these entrepreneurs knew from the beginning that they would end up in video. For others, it was an accident, a shot in the dark, yes, even an act of desperation.

Few would fit the image that observers have of entrepreneurs. "The model of the entrepreneur that everyone conjures up, of the promotionally oriented, socially extroverted person, is rarely the stereotype that you see," said Anthony Hoffman, director of corporate financing for Cralin & Co., a venture capital firm that finds money for fledgling businesses. "Most are conservative, almost dull, very methodical in what they do."

If you are thinking of getting into video, it may help for you to learn about the backgrounds of some successful entrepreneurs. After hearing what qualifications and interests these people possess, and after understanding what they went through to start their businesses, you may be better prepared to evaluate your own situation.

Most experts agree that successfully launching and operating a new business requires many qualifications and talents. At the top of everyone's list is possession of an entrepreneurial spirit. "All you have to be is an entrepreneur," said Joseph Ostrow, executive vice-president and director of communications services at Young & Rubicam Inc., a major New York advertising agency. "You don't have to be a technical expert. You don't even have to know how to use the camera."

Peter Diamandis, who launched several of his own businesses and now is president of CBS Publications, believes what is needed is courage. "You have to have guts, a devil-may-care attitude that says, 'Everyone else is doing it, I can do it, too.' "

One person who has guts is Joe O'Connell, who managed an incredible career switch from high school principal to operator of a video dating service with more than 1,500 members. Joe readily admitted that he had no technical knowledge of video when he started out. "I did a lot of reading and went to a lot of workshops," he recalled. "It wasn't complicated. You just have to be willing to learn."

Most video entrepreneurs agree that it is not necessary to be a technical wizard going in. But once you are operating the business, it is crucial that you learn enough to keep the business ahead of the competition. In some video businesses like video dating where rudimentary video skills may suffice, it isn't necessary to become as knowledgeable as a Hollywood cameraman. In other businesses, it is. Skip Winitsky, whose Washington, D.C.–based company, Media/Arts Management Associates, videotapes training films for industry and political commercials for candidates running for office, puts great stock in honing his creative skills. He warned that anyone competing with him for a job should be similarly armed. "You have to know your tools," he said. "An artist knows how to mix his own paints. It's very competitive and if you're not very good, even if your father owns Warner-Amex, you're not going to get very far."

Some who are making it in the business believe that it is becoming easier to develop that expertise. "The technology is more accessible than it was years ago when you needed to be an electrical engineer," said Eugene Marlow, president of Media Enterprises Inc., which is producing programming for cable TV. "Today all you have to do is have the money to plunk down for the equipment."

Lee Roy Kaminski, owner and president of KTV Consultants Inc., believes that enthusiasm is a necessary virtue. He also believes that it isn't crucial to know everything about everything. Oftentimes you *should* depend on the skills of others. "Everyone thinks that video is a megalomaniac's dream, that you do everything yourself," he said. "When you do everything yourself, it looks like that. Video is an ensemble medium. It takes a large group of people with individual craft skills."

One talent that can make up enormously for any lack of technical expertise is marketing and promotional skill. "The entrepreneur who has tremendous marketing skills is much better off, because he will stimulate and excite people he talks with sufficiently so they will do serious work on his project," said Tony Hoffman. "A guy who comes in might have the world's best idea, but if he can't explain it in compelling terms, he is compromised by that inability."

Many of those in video actually developed their skills while working in the advertising industry. Richard Love, who runs a small videotaping operation, has been an advertising director with Hi Gear tire and auto centers in Capitol Heights, Maryland, for twelve years. "My background is advertising, so doing ads and brochures is second nature to me," he noted. Fred Russo, who operates Video Taping Services in Easton, Connecticut, also worked in marketing and advertising before starting his own video business. "I had a good marketing background, so I knew how to market," he explained. "I put together the brochures and other things I needed to sell my service."

Joan Hendrickson, owner of the Georgetown Connection, a video dating service in Washington, D.C., found marketing skills she didn't know she had when it came time to prevent her business from going under. She took a business course at a local community college and discovered she loved marketing. "I love P.R. and promotion," she said. "The biggest thrill for me is getting that media hit." Joan has had several of those hits to rejoice over, including a stint on "The Phil Donahue Show," an appearance on Larry King's national radio show, and feature articles in the *Wall Street Journal* and the *Washington Post*.

It took a university course to tap Joan's skills. Many experts recommend taking courses to round out your talents and uncover hidden ones. "There are so many universities around and communications is becoming such a popular subject that I would think you could find an expert to help," said Joe Ostrow. However, he cautions prospective students to check over the professor's background to make sure that he actually worked in the field he claims to be an expert in.

Other skills may be transferable to the video field, depending upon the video business. Speech therapy, for example, is a natural background for someone helping to train people to appear on video. Maureen White, executive vice-president at Introlens, a video dating service, pointed out that she was a psychology major in college. "Everyone here has a background in psychology," she said. "It gives you the ability to sit and listen to what people say."

An entrepreneurial spirit is evident in most video people. Jim Perkins, who has led an independent business life most of his working days, did not realize that fact until quite recently. "I went back and did a reprise of my own career and discovered that whatever situation I got involved in, I started something new," he said.

Many video entrepreneurs did not plan to run a video business. Like Jim, they just wanted to do something new and different. Eugene Marlow was working as an editor on a trade publication after spending four years in the air force and then earning his MBA. He was looking for something new and, sensing the potential in video, took a job as a communications consultant with a major corporation. Along the way, he amassed knowledge and soon found himself heading up the video operation at Union Carbide. During his more than six years with the company, he built the video operation into a $4.5 million facility with fifteen people shooting fifty to sixty video projects a year.

Union Carbide executives asked Gene to conduct a detailed study of the cable TV industry so that the company could plot its own future course. During the study, Gene met many cable TV executives and began to learn which services were needed. The opportunity to start a company to fulfill those needs proved irresistible.

Dottie Nelson's future was altered one day when she saw Joan Hendrickson on "The Phil Donahue Show." At that time, Dottie was self-employed as a seamstress and free-lance artist. She wanted to change careers. She was also very interested in single people, since she noticed they had trouble meeting one another in Louisville, Kentucky, where she lived. Dottie traveled to Washington and paid Joan a consulting fee to learn how to set up and run a video dating service. Dottie's service now has more than 100 members.

Both Joe O'Connell, who launched People Resources in New York, and David Gresty, owner of Getting Together in Ft. Lauderdale, credit their involvement in video dating services to the fact that they got divorced and suddenly realized the plight of the newly single. "The only background you need for being single is being single," stated David.

Joe also confessed that he had always been fascinated by technical equipment. In fact, many of the video entrepreneurs fall into this category. Susan Dinter, owner of Vipro Communications Inc., a Philadelphia-based legal videotaping company, said that she was an avid photographer and interested in technology. She studied court reporting to earn money to put herself through college. "I enjoyed fixing the stenotype machine more than I enjoyed taking the stenotype down," she said. When she made that discovery, Susan "read everything I could get my hands on," to learn more about videotape.

In addition to his marketing and advertising experience, Fred Russo had worked as a photographer and had photographed weddings. He enjoyed the technical aspects of recording a wedding, and it was an easy transition from still photography to videotape. "I wanted to get into a growing industry, like computers were in the sixties and seventies," Fred explained. "I wanted to do creative work and use my talents. I wanted a people-oriented business."

John Phillips, owner of Video Replay in Westport, Connecticut, pointed out that he had a good technical and business background before he launched his own business. "I had managed three different video retail stores," he said. Although John attended the University of Miami and majored in mass communications, that background proved less useful than he had thought. "When I was in school, from the late sixties until 1973, the video explosion hadn't occurred, at least not to the degree it has now," he said. "My formal education is dated somewhat. Everything else I've learned is flying by the seat of my pants."

It seems that once a video entrepreneur decides what he wants to do, he must be persistent, even if the business takes a while to get off the ground. Jim Perkins noted that his first attempt to sell one of his cable ideas to a major cable company fell flat. "I couldn't get to see anybody of any importance," he said. "I finally got in to see someone. He said, 'I'll give you ten minutes,' and immediately answered the phone and talked for nine minutes and twenty seconds. Then he looked at his watch and said, 'I've got a meeting. Thanks for coming by.'"

But Jim did not give up. He eventually had better luck with the Modern Satellite Network, which agreed to give him satellite time for "The Home Shopping Show," where viewers could call up and order any of the merchandise being shown. Soon, he rounded up advertisers and talent and had the show on cable TV. "It was a matter of not knowing enough about what I was getting into, so the potential consequences were not a deterrent," he laughed. "I was too dumb to know any better." Jim, dumb luck and all, was able to sell "The Home Shopping Show" to MSN for a very tidy profit.

Carol Slatkin, a partner in Spectra Video Services in Washington, D.C., was no less persistent in getting her career off the ground. Carol grew up in a darkroom and always knew she would end up in photography or film. In college she took a course in video and was determined to make it her field.

For several years after graduating from college she was unable to find work, even as a production assistant. But she did unpaid work in community video in New York, borrowing equipment from the city to work with ghetto groups. She did it for the experience, hoping to turn her volunteer work into a paying job. She ended up moving to Washington doing press work for the Smithsonian Institution. Along the way she joined two film organizations, where she made valuable contacts.

Carol finally landed a job as a production assistant with two people who were shooting video for corporations. While with that group, she worked with a free-lance photographer who shared Carol's dream of having his own business. The two of them struck out on their own and started Spectra Video. They now do video work for many unions in Washington, as well as industry associations. Carol strongly recommends joining local organizations in order to meet people working in the industry. She does not minimize what it took to get her where she is now. "I worked very hard," she said.

Lee Kaminski also knew he would wind up doing something in film or video. His early years, in fact, were spent before the camera. As a child, Lee appeared in numerous commercials for products like Kraft margarine and Kellogg's cereals. While he was leading the life of a TV star at an early age, Lee also was deeply influenced by his parents, both of whom had scientific backgrounds. He knew that he wanted to work in TV, but behind the camera, not in front of it.

Today, Lee trains other TV professionals to work with videotape. Along the way, Lee has done just about everything imaginable in the medium, including taping such events as fashion shows for later play by department stores and performances at Lincoln Center in New York City for the center's archives.

Lee is a firm believer in volunteering until a paying job comes along. If a video person develops a rapport with someone who is working regularly but may not have enough money to pay well, it is worthwhile to help out as a volunteer. When the person can afford to, said Lee, he will want to pay you.

Lee believes that a basic talent for video is needed, but he also credits dedication. "You have to say 'I can do it,' and then do it to your own satisfaction," he said.

Like Carol, who took Lee's advice and did volunteer work, Nelson Martinez made his own breaks along the way. Nelson was working for a TV station in San Antonio, but wasn't satisfied with the amount of time he was getting on the air. So he took on extra jobs whenever the station needed an extra camera crew to shoot something. "That's how I started to do free-lance work," he said. "Back then I wasn't getting paid anything."

Nelson was particularly interested in covering the activities of the Hispanic community. "I started doing that on my own, filming their cultural events, their dances, anything that happened in the community."

A producer at the TV station was always looking for filler—two- or three-minute segments that could help to fill up airtime. She told Nelson that she couldn't authorize any overtime, but would encourage him to shoot and edit a story, and she would supply the copy. Nelson's segments, which included spots on flamenco dancers, a Salsa fashion show, and Puerto Rican artists, began to attract attention. Eventually he had more free-lance work than he could cope with, so he left his job to strike out on his own. Today, Nelson does not work for free. He has branched out and now videotapes weddings and other special events, as well as tackling the more professionally demanding job of shooting commercials. He proudly describes his company: "It's a real live functioning business."

While some video people like Carol, Lee, and Nelson decided early on that video was for them, others fall into it by accident. Joan Hendrickson's entry into the video dating business was one such accident. Joan got divorced, and because she had never held a paying job, had no work experience. She took an interviewing job with a newly founded video dating service in Washington, D.C., out of desperation. She soon discovered to her amazement that the job fit like a glove.

Skip Winitsky is someone else who discovered video when he began to doubt his first career choice, law. "I was walking down a hallway at college and saw a room filled with equipment," he recalled. "I went in and talked with the guy working in there and he turned out to be a film teacher. Shortly after that, I started to study photography."

As most of these video entrepreneurs demonstrate, you have to be dedicated and willing to work hard. "You have to be driven to do it, either because you want to be a star or because you want to work on your own," said Skip. "A lot of people in this business like the autonomy and creativity."

Before you decide to start a video business, there are

some negatives to consider, especially if you are now working in a safe, comfortable job with a regular yearly salary, a secretary, and a well-furnished office. The fear of failure is very real and must be dealt with. "Being a small entrepreneur unsuccessfully is probably one of the most painful experiences you can have in your life," said Peter Diamandis.

In the beginning, getting by without all the support systems afforded by working for a company can be traumatic. "Do you realize I have two hundred people around me who handle day-to-day details," said Peter, gesturing around the offices at CBS. "I don't know who does it, but it gets done."

For a small entrepreneur, "When it's working, it's very pleasant, but when it's not working, it's pretty painful," said Peter. "You're ducking your creditors."

Yet Peter is one who talks with fondness about his days as an entrepreneur. "Being successful is marvelous," he said. "You make more money than anyone else. There are literally hundreds of thousands of entrepreneurs who make $500,000 each year. They're building up enormous equity. You find out that at age sixty these guys can write a check for $10 million or $20 million when they sell their companies."

It is that possibility that has inspired many an entrepreneur. And because video is such an exciting and growing new field, a great many of these entrepreneurs are finding themselves in this industry.

But aside from the money, these video entrepreneurs have launched their own businesses for other reasons, and the reasons are as diverse as the types of businesses they have started. For Carol Slatkin, it fulfills her need to do something that is issue-oriented, that allows her to express her own beliefs in ways unthought of before. "We did a tape showing union people who were out on strike and struggling," she recalled. "We were able to show them as families, not as people throwing rocks and stones. The union was able to use the tape to enlist support for its cause."

But aside from working for various causes, Carol enjoys video because it is interesting and exciting. "Even if you spend some time in the editing room, you get to be in different places all the time," she said enthusiastically. "Yesterday I was shooting union recruiters at a fish fry in Cleveland, Tennessee. The day before I was in the office of the executive director of the Wilderness Society, who has the most incredible collection of Ansel Adams prints. I am always meeting fascinating people."

Gene Marlow admitted that he works at his business, Media Enterprises, seven days a week. "I make one mistake a day, and sometimes I'm filled with anxiety," he said. "But all my options are open and that's a wonderful feeling."

For Joan Hendrickson, the Georgetown Connection has fulfilled her career aspirations. She is working for herself, becoming well known as an authority on single people, and having a good time to boot. "Moreover, I really think I'm doing the best thing for the type of personality I have," she said. She is doing meaningful work, helping single people meet other single people. She has wonderful stories to tell about the people she has met and helped. "I had a blind woman come in with her Seeing Eye dog," Joan recalled. "She lost her eyesight in the car accident that killed her husband. My first inclination was to tell her I couldn't help her. But I couldn't turn her away, either. I did a tape of her and told some of my clients about her—she's studying to be a professor of law. I was excited by the response. Several of my clients wanted to meet her and she made some very good friends. She still comes to our parties and has become a good friend of mine."

Of course this is just a sampling of the many people who

are involved in video today. But even from this small sample, you can see that video entrepreneurs are a disparate group. That is part of what makes video so exciting. It is attracting men and women of different backgrounds, interests, and talents. Each has something unique to offer.

Are you one of these people? Do you have what it takes to make a career in video?

Only you can answer that question, but here are some factors to consider:

- Are you a self-starter? Can you devise a plan of action and then carry it out by yourself?
- Are you willing to take responsibility? Can you make decisions quickly if needed?
- Do you work well with others? Would you be comfortable in the role of manager?
- Are you a good communicator? Do you say what you mean and mean what you say? Will clients, employees, and others be able to accept you at your word?
- Are you in good health? Do you have energy left over at the end of the day?
- Are you willing to work more than an eight-hour day to get your business going and to keep it going?
- Are you willing to learn new skills, possibly going through a workshop or training course?
- Are you comfortable with new technology?
- Are you excited about the potential of video? Do you have enough enthusiasm to be able to sell other people on your idea?
- Do you often think of new uses for video that might make your job easier?
- Do you have enough of a financial cushion to support yourself and your new venture until it gets off the ground?

· Will you stick with your business and not lose interest if it doesn't take off immediately?

If you can answer yes to most of these questions, then you should be thinking about starting a video business. Remember that you can test the waters before leaping in. You might want to start by working at your new career on weekends, perhaps videotaping weddings. If you find you are not suited to this new career, then you will not have abandoned your other job and at least will have satisfied your own curiosity about video.

But if the business starts to grow, and you find (wonder of wonders!) you also are having a good time, then video is for you.

2

The Sky's the Limit

SOME EXPERTS see the video revolution ripping through society with hurricane force, uprooting conventional ways and sweeping aside anyone who resists. It is unlikely, however, that video will shake up our world overnight. Change will occur gradually as we recognize video's potential for enabling us to work more efficiently and enjoy life more fully. Over time, various video innovations will be taken for granted and we will wonder how we ever got along without them.

In the long term, there will be no limit to the number of businesses that could be affected by video. When Joseph Ostrow, executive vice-president and director of communications services for Young & Rubicam Inc., was asked about future uses for video, his response was: "How much time do you have?" Joe then proceeded to list dozens of areas where video might play a role.

But unless you are endowed with prophetic powers, you will not be able to predict with great certainty how we will use video twenty years from now. You may find your inability to predict the future extremely frustrating. You are not alone. "We're all part of an intellectual chain," explained Jim

Perkins, one video pioneer. "Our minds allow us to go from link to link, but we are limited by that chain. We can't get to link three until we get to link two. And we're all wondering what's on link four." Jim offers the perfect example to illustrate his thought. Before the automobile was invented, who could have predicted the profit potential in parking garages?

Similarly, who knows what will happen in the next decade that will impact video? Already experts are talking about combining video with computer technology, thus increasing video's applicability. Or totally new technologies could come along that could interface with video. Such developments could open up opportunities never before envisioned.

For your own purposes, however, you should not be too eager to see into the future. Your concern is the present. You must worry about the immediate marketability of your video idea.

Timing is crucial. You want to be ahead of the crowd so that your use for video will be recognized as exciting and unique. But unless you have the resources and patience to wait for years until your idea catches on, you must hit on a concept that will succeed now.

How will you come up with such an idea?

You could hope that a vision will come to you while you sleep. And, indeed, that could very well happen. Each of us has, at one time or another, looked at a new product or invention that is successful and also is fairly simple, and thought: "Why didn't I think of that?" While the solution might seem simple, getting there was the battle. Chances are that the innovator knew a lot about the subject. It also is likely that he had encountered a specific problem and was seeking a solution. His new product idea was the result.

One day soon, you may be struck with the greatest idea

for video ever. But before that happens, you will have to learn a lot more about video. Your research should begin the moment you decide you are interested in starting a video business. From that time on, you should become the most observant member of your group. You should constantly be watching, recording, and gathering information that could lead to a salable idea.

Your ears should perk up every time you hear the word "video." Read the business press as well as the specialized video magazines. "Constantly read as much of the trade press as possible," advised David M. Simons, president of Digital Video Corp., which advises buinesses on uses for new electronic technology. "It will be a great stimulation to your imagination."

Clip articles that you find particularly intriguing. Seek out more information on those stories. Get in touch with the person whose byline appears on the piece. Often, the writer will have additional information that could not be included in the story because of space restrictions. He might be able to send you some of this material.

Do you feel that someone quoted as an expert in one of these articles may have more to say on the subject? Why not try to contact that individual to begin a dialogue? Don't assume that these experts are unapproachable. Most love to talk about what they do and are flattered when someone expresses a great interest in their opinions.

Your best strategy would be to send this person a letter (to his business address if you know it, or in care of the publication where he was quoted) in which you compliment him on his insightful comments, then go on to pose another question or two. Tell him something about yourself—your education, your employment history, and why you are interested in video. Explain that you are eager to meet and talk with him to benefit from his expertise. Suggest that you meet for lunch or coffee. Be sure to include your address and phone number.

The expert is bound to be pleased by your remarks and will be inclined to answer your letter. Even if you don't succeed in setting up a meeting with him but merely chat on the phone or exchange letters, you will have established a contact that you can use in the future. Even during a brief encounter, you will collect information that you can add to your total knowledge of video. It is possible that this expert will refer you to other people who can help you.

Your quest for a hot video idea is not unlike an investor's search for a hot stock. Those who are ignorant of the stock market are inclined to think that those who make money are just plain lucky. Of course, in anything involving speculation there is a certain amount of luck involved. But more often than not the investor has done his homework. He studies the market and the various companies. He learns about different industries.

You can make use of some of his methods. Learn as much as you can about companies involved in video. If the company is a public company and issues an annual report, arrange to get a copy.

An annual report will include all the pertinent financial statistics on a company, including its revenues and profits. But this report also will discuss the company's strategy for growth. If the company has a video project on the drawing boards, chances are it will be discussed in the annual report.

Obviously, you will not have the resources to go out and start a competing business first. But finding out what the larger companies are doing will help you formulate your own game plan. You can see which areas they see as hot ones for video.

In addition to annual reports, keep a special eye out for newspaper and magazine stories on media and entertainment companies. Often these articles, especially if they are lengthy and analytical, will include comments from some chief executive as he speculates on the future of his company. That assessment is likely to include video.

When a major corporation looks for new products, it very often will employ focus groups. These are gatherings of ordinary consumers who sit around and discuss various new products, why they would use them (or not use them), and what other new products they would like to see come onto the market. Companies usually pay large sums to conduct such research. You can employ the same methods without spending a dime.

Try to put together a well-informed group of people from among your friends and business associates. Invite them over for an evening. If it's a small group, you could arrange dinner; with a larger crowd, cocktails or coffee and dessert.

Toss out a few of your own ideas and comments and then listen to what other people have to offer. What you will have is a brainstorming session where thoughts and ideas get thrown around, embellished, knocked down, and built up again. These get-togethers are common in many creative environments where writers, artists, and others feel they need to talk over their thoughts with colleagues. Such a session will get your own creative juices flowing.

Keep an open mind. In the beginning, you don't want to rule out anything. Wait to form your opinions until you have all the facts. When you are with others, do more listening than talking. Your goal is to learn. Also, if you do have good ideas, you want to be the one to implement them, not give them away.

Wherever you are, ask people what they do. Without appearing to be putting them through the third degree, determine whether they use video in their jobs. If not, are there ways that video might be employed to make their jobs easier? Ask them what they find frustrating about their work. Have they thought about ways new technology could lighten the load?

Be more observant in your own life. When you are on the job, really think about what you do. Break down every task, step by step. Is there anything that you do at work that could be helped by video? What about at home? Are there normal everyday tasks that you or your family perform that could be altered by video? Look at your recreational activities. Is there a new way that video could enhance your social life?

You are looking for any problems that you or someone else might encounter in the office or at home. Once you have identified a problem, you can determine whether video might provide a solution. "Always think in terms of the problems that people have," said Dave Simons. "Most things that are successful are ways of doing something better than it's already being done."

Video can improve upon existing methods. "With anything that is enhanced by being seen and heard, video has the opportunity for making a place for itself," said Richard Love, a video entrepreneur in Maryland.

Indeed, video already is finding its niche. During the past few years, video entrepreneurs from all over the United States have been discovering new applications and developing successful businesses. "There is a flurry of activity to find consumer uses," observed Gregory W. Blaine, director of new communication technologies at Foote, Cone & Belding.

The second half of this book will discuss some specific businesses in depth to demonstrate how these videographers got started. Each person is unique and brings to video his own thoughts, talents, and energies. As you will see from the later examples, many of the successful videographers started out in other careers but found themselves attracted to video.

It is hoped that these illustrations will stimulate your own thinking, because with video the sky is the limit on what you can achieve. "Video could be used to solve almost any type of problem," said Steve Lokker, manager for employee communications for Pratt & Whitney, a division of United Technologies Corp. "The application is limited only by the imagination of the people who control it."

3

Will My Idea Sell?

ONE DAY you will be out walking the dog when, eureka! you come up with a great idea for a video business. Of course you think it's a great idea, but how do you find out for sure? All new ventures are risky, but video carries with it an even higher degree of risk. After all, many of these new video businesses have never been marketed before. You may have no other company's track record to study and may be in the position of creating a whole new market for your product or service. Can you do it? Is the world ready for your video business?

No company worth its stock price on Wall Street would introduce a new product or service without first doing extensive research and market testing. Sometimes even with such preparation, a product will fail. Nothing is foolproof. But after doing some research, you will at least have a better idea of your chances for success. "Research is critical to any of these undertakings," said Joseph Ostrow.

You do not have the financial or human resources of a Procter & Gamble or General Foods. Nonetheless, you can do a respectable research job on your own for little cost using many resources at your disposal. "People underestimate the research sources obtainable through libraries and associations," said Henry A. Kaplan, an executive vice-president at CBS.

This is not the time to solicit personal opinions from brother Harold or grandpa Pete. Not unless these relatives know a lot about video, marketing, or advertising, or happen to be members of the group you propose to sell to. It is unlikely that you will get an objective, informed opinion. "People often rely on the opinions of relatives or friends. It's a big mistake," said David M. Simons, president of Digital Video Corp. "You have to do research and testing. It's worth the effort."

After the initial euphoria over your idea wears off, try to step back and look at it objectively. Listen to the guidelines used by Anthony Hoffman, director of corporate financing for Cralin & Co., Inc., a venture capital firm that finances new businesses: "Does it make sense as a business? Will it succeed? Is it something unique? Patentable? Can I sell it to investors? It has to have a sizzle or a hook, something that gives it an unusually high chance of succeeding."

Keep in mind that merely adding video to an existing service may not result in a marketable product. "Some people feel that everything that is now audio turned into video will be a tremendous business opportunity," said Tony Hoffman. "But there are some functions that audio alone is good for. You have to look at each idea independently."

When evaluating the potential of a video business, you should avoid one pitfall. Remember that the consumer will be buying a service, not the technology. "Separate your attachment to the technology from the business idea itself," cautions Dave Simons. "You have to look at what the consumer sees. The consumer doesn't see the technology. He sees what it means to him. People don't care about what the medium is. They care about the advantages." You have to show why your service is better than the one a consumer may have access to already.

It also is crucial that you are able to explain your service to the average consumer. Get personal. Explain what the service will mean to the individual. Avoid technical terms.

Your first task is to determine who your customer would be. If you are thinking of opening up a video dating service in your hometown, you are aiming at a single adult market, aged thirty years and older. You are going to go after people who are fairly urbane, as opposed to those living in rural areas. How many of these people exist in your area?

The best way to find out is to obtain the latest data from the Census Bureau. This information should be readily available through your nearest public library. If not, then you can write or call the Census Bureau in Washington, D.C.

If you find that there are very few people in your target area that fit into the single adult category, then perhaps you need to find another location or another business. If, however, the census data confirms your hunch that there is a large single population in your own backyard, then you know that you have a group of potential customers for your service.

Now that you know there is a potential market for your service, you must find out whether there is a need for it. Perhaps the easiest way to find out is to ask some single people you already know. It isn't necessary for you to go into great detail about the service you are thinking of offering. A better approach would be to let these single people do the talking. Do these professional men and women have trouble meeting people with similar backgrounds and interests? Where do they now go? Are they pleased with the types of people they are meeting? Are they looking for an easier way to find dates?

In asking these questions, you will be gathering information that not only will help you identify your market, but also will enable you to design your own service to fit your customer's needs. This is not unlike the research Joe O'Connell did before he launched People Resources in New York City. Joe, who had been recently divorced, visited a few singles bars to meet eligible women and found this method of finding dates was not to his liking He also discovered that many other people who frequented the same bars felt the same way he did. It wasn't long afterward that Joe hit on the idea of People Resources.

Visit singles bars and talk to people. Also solicit the opinions of the single people who live in your apartment building or work in your office. Ask these single people whether they have ever used a dating service and, if so, what their impressions were. This not only will give you clues as to how to improve upon existing services, but will give you an idea of the competition.

Visit the competition and learn as much as you can. "See what you have to do to be better," said CBS's Henry Kaplan.

If the first steps in your research show that you have a large enough group of potential customers, and that they need a good dating service, the next question is, will a video dating service meet that need?

The best way to answer that question is to determine whether people are disillusioned with the dating services now available to them, and if so, why. Do these dating services match people up without giving the client a choice in the matter? Some computer dating services presume to tell clients which person is the best match. What looks good on paper, however, may not work in real life. Your service would allow the customer to choose his or her own dates, so that would be an improvement. But perhaps the major difference would be that your clients would be given a "sneak preview" of each candidate. It is one thing to read a person's background on a piece of paper; it is quite another to hear and see that person talk about himself on videotape.

After going through this step-by-step assessment, you will probably conclude that a video dating service would be a vast improvement over existing services. It provides single people with the most dignified, most efficient, least painful way of meeting new people.

Once you have demonstrated that a video dating service would be better than the other services now offered, you must determine whether people who need your service will buy it. Answering that question is a difficult task. Here you are dealing with people's attitudes, and it is impossible to get an accurate reading. Often a consumer's willingness to buy does not translate into an actual sale. Many companies have been fooled by the fickle public. Major corporations will do surveys asking people whether they would buy a certain product, and they often will say yes. But when those same customers are in the supermarket, they may change their minds. Thus the research was worth nil.

So how do you find out whether a single person in your community would pay $100 or more to join a video dating service?

Again the easiest way may be to ask a few single people. "It's a mini test market," said Alvin Hampel, chairman of D'Arcy-MacManus & Masius in New York. "You've got to get a typical prospect and try out things on that person, or on two or three persons, to see what you're doing right or wrong. Nothing will help more than that."

Remember one important fact when evaluating a consumer service: You are a consumer, too. "One nice thing about video is that most of the products are consumer products and services so you can make a judgment as a consumer whether it's a good idea. You don't have to put yourself in the shoes of a corporate buyer," noted Tony Hoffman. Even Tony admits, "I always feel much more confident if I'm evaluating the response of a consumer than of a purchasing agent in a major corporation." So how do you honestly feel about the business you are proposing? Would you be a customer?

As you may already have realized, research alone can never provide all the answers on whether your business will succeed. Peter Diamandis, president of CBS Publications, who has started several businesses during his career, noted that determining what will sell is a combination of experience and judgment. Experience is something you must earn, while "judgment is something that is God-given," Peter said. "It's a rare commodity."

If your research paints a positive picture and you have a good feeling about your idea, then chances are good you will succeed. "You have to follow your instincts," advised Jim Perkins, whose own instincts led him to start the successful cable TV venture "The Home Shopping Show."

What if your target clients were a professional group, lawyers or real estate dealers for example? How do you determine whether there is a market?

The process is pretty much the same as for a video dating service. The difference will be in the information sources you use. In some cases, evaluating a video business aimed at business is easier. If you can prove that your service can get the job done faster and cheaper than conventional methods, you are on solid ground. You will be able to develop a rationale for your service, one that many businesses will find hard to ignore.

As with assessing the consumer market, you must first ascertain that there are enough customers for your service in your area. If you are thinking of setting up a video legal service, for example, you must determine whether there are enough lawyers around to make up a potential market. There are several ways of finding out the size of your local legal community. Check with the local bar association, which might keep such statistics. Another good information source is *Martindale-Hubbell Law Directory*. Lawyers pay to be listed in this reference book so the listings may not be complete. Still, you know that any figure it gives on the legal population in a given area would be the minimum. *Martindale-Hubbell* is available in most library reference sections.

Probably one of the best sources for a listing of lawyers in your area is the Yellow Pages. This section of the phone book also would be a good way to find out the number of real estate agents, doctors, or other professional group.

Once you determine that there are enough professionals in your area to make up a good market for your service, you should conduct your own survey to assess their needs. You can start by talking with professional people that you know. At some point, it will be necessary to seek the opinions of a more formal group. This is where local associations will come in handy. The local bar association or a local organization of real estate agents would be excellent places to start.

Don't be afraid of calling on some of these professionals personally to solicit their opinions. The best approach would be to send a letter in which you include some of the details of your idea and ask for an appointment to discuss your thoughts further. Be sure to make clear in the letter the advantages your service would offer to this profession.

When you visit professional people make sure you are prepared. Most of them have busy schedules and will be annoyed if you just come in to bounce ideas around. Before your appointment with any such individual, do your homework on his business. Perhaps your idea is to videotape homes for sale so that a real estate agent could show these tapes to prospective clients in his office rather than driving them around town. Make sure you know which territories the agent works in. Must he drive his prospects on highways that are often congested? You might even try driving his route and clocking it so you can tell him exactly how much time he is using to chauffeur his customers around. Include other statistics—gasoline, car maintenance, highway and bridge tolls. Going through this exercise, you can come up with a good idea of how much money a video service could save him.

Make sure, however, that you don't presume to tell these professionals how to do their job. Anyone would be irritated by a pushy salesperson who talks as if he knows everything about a job he has never worked at. Remember, you also are there to solicit this professional's thoughts. People like to talk about what they do. Draw each person out. Find out what it is about his job that he finds frustrating. Perhaps it is something that video can make easier.

A key ingredient is pricing your service not only so that you can make a reasonable profit, but also so that your customers can afford the service. A video dating service may be a great idea, but if you have to charge each person $1,000 in order to pay your bills, you are doomed before you start.

If you have competitors, find out what they are charging. It isn't always necessary that you charge less. After all, your service will be the better one, right? But those figures will give you a ballpark estimate.

There are several variables to consider when pricing a service. First, your own costs and what you expect to make as a profit. Second, how many customers you can reasonably expect to sign up. Balancing out the two will help you decide whether you can price your service so it will sell.

As you will learn in chapter 7, it is impossible to prevent others from copying your idea for a video business. Therefore, until you can get your idea off the ground, try not to let everyone in the world know what you are up to. Even if your video idea is not unique, improvements you are planning may be. You do not want someone else opening up a competing business before you have time to sign a lease. You want to have the advantage of being first.

But don't let that fact cause you to rush into a new business before you are certain it is a good move. You have more to lose by jumping in before you have done all your research and concluded your idea is a sound one. That reassurance will give you the extra confidence you will need during those trying times in the beginning weeks and months.

4

How to Market, Advertise, and Sell

YOU MAY have the best video idea ever, produce the best product imaginable, and be one of the most innovative people in the business. But unless you know how to advertise and market your service, it is unlikely that you will meet with great success. For that, you have to create public awareness of your product. Perhaps you will never become a household name like Frank Perdue, but with a sound advertising plan, you *can* reach the people who count—your potential customers.

Chances are, if you are just starting out, you will not have thousands of dollars to spend running your commercials during the Super Bowl. Actually, network television would not be the best advertising medium for you anyway. You are interested in reaching customers who live within your area. And there are many advertising media, some relatively inexpensive, that will suit your needs perfectly.

When you think of advertising you probably think of TV, radio, magazines, and newspapers. Indeed, these are all important advertising vehicles that you may very well want to take advantage of. But there are others—direct mail, pennysavers, Yellow Pages, for example—that you should not overlook. In fact, any device that keeps your service in the public eye will serve the purpose.

Sponsor a Little League team? Why not? For the small cost of buying uniforms and ice cream cones after the game, you can have dozens of adorable children running around a ball field and town with the name of your company emblazoned on their backs. Not only will it get your name around, but it certainly won't hurt your public image.

Use your imagination and use your community contacts. Constantly evaluate your advertising plan and be flexible enough to make changes if necessary.

As a first step, you must develop a positive attitude about advertising. Too many entrepreneurs regard it as optional. Nothing could be farther from the truth. Advertising is crucial to your business. "You can't exist without it," emphasized Joe O'Connell, who started People Resources, a video dating service in New York, and now is vice-president of Winner Communications, a New York advertising agency.

Advertising is as important to the success of your business as the equipment you will buy. And just as you budgeted for that equipment, you must budget for advertising. With your equipment, you will constantly be adding new pieces and paying to maintain what you own. The same is true of advertising—it will be an ongoing expense.

While you will want to keep your expenses in line, remember that people are attracted to bargains. Special incentives, introductory discounts, and contests may cost you something, but can help to build the business, especially when you are starting out.

Just as McDonald's watches Burger King and Coke watches Pepsi, you will want to watch your competitors so that you may counter their advertising campaigns. In fact, your advertising strategy will be greatly influenced by your competition. "You define what league you want to play in," said Gregory W. Blaine, director of new communication technologies at Foote, Cone & Belding Communications, Inc. "If it's the major league, then you have to play like a major leaguer. If not, just don't think that you're going to make the World Series."

There is no hard and fast rule about how much you should be spending on advertising. Spend enough to get the job done. Also keep in mind that spending a large amount will not necessarily mean increased business. You are looking for the most efficient advertising medium—one that reaches the largest number of potential customers for the least cost—and you may have to do a good deal of experimenting before you hit on the right media mix that will work for you.

How will you discover whether your advertising scheme is working? Well, Joan Hendrickson, owner of the Georgetown Connection, a video dating service in Washington, D.C., makes it a point to ask each new customer how he or she heard about the business. That way, Joan has a record of which advertising vehicles are producing customers.

People are fascinated with video. Take advantage of that fascination when selling your service. "It's probably easier to get your foot in the door with the magic of video because you're dealing with something that everyone is interested in and fascinated with," said Alvin Hampel, chairman of D'Arcy-MacManus & Masius in New York. Many customers will be easy to sell because they are always looking for something new and different to enhance their leisure activities or to increase their efficiency.

One word of caution, however. While video can be a major selling point for you, remember that some of your potential customers may be apprehensive. "If you're marketing something to the baby boom generation on up, you'd better include something to overcome their anxiety," said Greg Blaine. Some people, for example, may be terrified by the idea of making a videotape for a video dating service. You must do your best to reassure them. Don't start your business by scaring people off with technological jargon or statements that sound farfetched.

Where should you advertise? It seems like an awesome problem. But with a little research and planning you can conquer it.

Remember all the information you gathered when you were trying to decide whether your idea would sell? A lot of that data will come in very handy now.

When you were solving that problem, you began by identifying your customer. That is also your first task here. Perhaps you are setting up a consumer business and plan to videotape weddings, bar mitzvahs, and parties. It is fairly obvious who would be good prospects for your service. Now your task is to find the advertising media that will reach these people.

Before you begin to investigate advertising media that cost money, be sure to take advantage of those that don't. Many stores—supermarkets, dry cleaners, and drug stores—have community bulletin boards where they allow customers to tack up notices and advertisements. This neighborhood classified section is a great place for you to start.

Don't scribble your notice on a leftover piece of cardboard. Make it look attractive and professional. Be sure your location and phone number are prominently stated. You may even want to attach to your large poster smaller pieces of paper that contain all the pertinent information about your business. The potential customers can tear these off and take them home.

If approached in the proper manner, even stores that don't have bulletin boards may be willing to display your advertisement. Here you may want to zero in on businesses that also provide services for weddings and parties. Bakeries, for example, will be taking orders for wedding cakes, and since your service is not competition for them, might be willing to help you advertise. Bridal shops, florists, tuxedo rental shops, jewelers, printers, and beauty salons all are places that will be frequented by young people with wedding bells in their future. To reach people who are thinking of throwing a party, try delicatessens or gourmet food stores that might cater the event, and also liquor stores.

When you are approaching other businesses to help you advertise, don't overlook those that may, on the surface at least, appear to be competitors. Still photographers, for example, make a good chunk of their income by photographing weddings. Yet most people who want their weddings videotaped also want still photographs. So work in concert with these photographers, not against them. Many still photographers have resisted getting into video themselves, but often are asked to provide such a service to their clients. If they know about your service, they can recommend you.

Remember that people who frequent camera and video stores are good sales prospects for you, too. Many of these hobbyists have an intense interest in video, but may not have the time or talent to actually videotape one of their own events. If the proprietors of these stores know about your work, they will want to mention your services to their customers. Introduce yourself to these shopkeepers and offer to show them samples of your work.

If you know that one particular business in your community reaches a great many people who would be perfect customers for your video service, you may want to do more than just place your poster in the window. The ideal situation would be to have the proprietor of this business become one of your fans so that he will enthusiastically recommend your service to his own customers.

What will it take to get him on your team? Well, if he's

not the second cousin of your third cousin Bernie, and if he isn't in debt to your father, then the best way is to offer to barter. Bartering—trading goods or services without the exchange of money—works best in these situations. Perhaps this proprietor has a son or daughter who is getting married, being confirmed, or graduating from high school. Why not offer to videotape this event for free in return for his endorsement? If you are just starting out, you may need a few sample videotapes to entice other customers. So, really, you have little to lose and everything to gain.

You may also think about using bartering in another manner. If you are having trouble writing or drawing an advertisement that captures the spirit of your business, you may have thought about hiring a professional to do the job for you. But you know even before you price such a service that you could never afford it. Still, you can probably locate an advertising genius within your own community who would agree to help you out in exchange for a few hours of your time. Perhaps he would like the contents of his home videotaped for insurance purposes. Or maybe he's giving a fiftieth anniversary party for his parents and would like the event videotaped.

You should try to obtain the business of community groups and associations like the Knights of Columbus. Offer to videotape some of their social gatherings, in order to bring your service to the attention of the members. It might be a good idea to think about offering special rates to members of these organizations just to court their business.

Your videotape, of course, should include your title and credits, with your address and phone number. After seeing a sample of your work, individual members may seek you out for other jobs. "Every job I've done, I've met someone else who led to another job," said John Fama, president of Famavision and Fama II Productions in New York. John even makes it a practice to pass out his business cards to interested onlookers when one of his production companies is videotaping on the street.

If you are offering to videotape sports events, there are several ways for you to bring your service to the attention of those who count. Raymond A. McArdle, media director for the New York advertising agency D'Arcy-MacManus & Masius, suggests that you locate the appropriate people in local schools, sports leagues, bowling alleys, and the like and seek to become the "official video service of . . ." In that manner, you might attract the attention of parents who may have other jobs for you to do.

When searching for sporting opportunities, don't forget local country clubs, tennis courts, and golf courses. There might be opportunities in any of these areas for you to make instructional tapes. Perhaps some student would like to be videotaped so that he can view his progress. There might also be a chance to videotape tournaments and outings.

During the 1983 New York City Marathon, one video company arranged to videotape each entrant crossing the finish line. Anyone who ran in the marathon and finished could later buy a videotape that included not only his final lunge over the finish line but also scenes showing the 17,165 runners starting on the Verrazano-Narrows Bridge and running more than 26 miles through the city's five boroughs. Perhaps there is a special sports event planned for your area that you could videotape. You would be paid for each videotape you sold and the resulting publicity could lead to other jobs.

Once you have exhausted your sources for free advertising, you should begin to investigate those that are low cost but effective. Direct mail is one good way for you to get your sales message to the people who count.

When a major company plans a mailing, it may spend

thousands of dollars purchasing a list of potential customers from another firm. You don't have to spend a fortune, but what you will have to spend is time to compile this list of your prospects yourself.

If you are marketing a real estate video service, for example, go through the Yellow Pages and make a list of those agents in your area who should receive your mailing. For a service that videotapes social events, you can make up a list of those planning weddings by searching the engagement section of your local newspapers or listings in local church bulletins. If you can obtain it, a list of those couples who have registered their china patterns in local department stores also would be a good source. Synagogues usually have records of young boys and young girls who will have bar and bas mitzvahs.

Once you have a list of possible clients, you can plan a mailing, targeting those individuals who are definitely in need of your service. Your job is to convince them, through a mailing, that they want your service.

Sound impossible? Not really. Just remember the times you were convinced, through the mail, to buy something. If you can recall why those solicitations impressed you, perhaps you can incorporate some of that approach into your own mailing.

Chances are the mailing that impressed you was very attractive, neat, and worded in a manner that caused you to respond positively. Make sure your mailing looks professional. Handwritten notes, dirty envelopes, and grammatical errors turn people off. If you can't afford to have your notice printed, then type it neatly and have it reproduced so that the copies look as good as the original. Hunt around until you find a photocopying machine that will give you the quality you want.

Your goal is to get each person to open your letter and not

toss it out with the so-called junk mail. How do you accomplish that? Experts say the best way is to handwrite rather than type each envelope. "It encourages readership and sets your mailing apart from other business mail," said Ray McArdle.

The packaging is important, but what about the contents? What are you going to say in your mailing to draw people to your door? Making the letter personal—in tone, message, and appearance—is the best approach. The ideal mailing would be a personal letter with a typed salutation to each individual. That could be time-consuming unless you have access to an electronic typewriter where you can change each greeting and then print out each letter.

But you can still achieve a personal tone by the way you word your letter. Here is an example for a consumer video business:

Dear Mr. Smith: [*salutation optional*]

After all the months of planning, the wedding day will seem to fly by. All those wonderful events—the bride walking down the aisle, the couple exchanging their vows, dancing the first waltz, and cutting the cake—will soon be just memories. If only there was a way to capture those moments forever.

Now there is. You can preserve that eventful day on videotape. Video Forever will capture every precious moment—from the preparations at the bride's home, through the wedding ceremony, and on to the reception—in full color and sound.

Think of what it will mean to your family and friends. When the honeymoon is over, you can have your friends over for a party to see themselves on TV. You can show the tape to those who were unable to attend. Imagine what fun it will be to show the tape to your grandchildren, years from now.

Our videographers are professional and unobtrusive. You will hardly know they are there until later when you view the fruits of their labors. If you would like to see a sampling of our work, we would be more than happy to schedule a private screening for you.

Best regards,
Robert Jones
President
Video Forever

Be sure to include your address and phone number. After a respectable amount of time has elapsed, you can follow up your mailing with phone calls.

You can also use the idea behind direct mail without using the mails. If you are able to single out a neighborhood filled with potential clients, you can distribute flyers—sheets of paper on which you have written your advertising message. The copy can be similar to the letter you mailed out, or you may want to have a larger heading to really catch people's eyes. These flyers can be left in mailboxes or on the windows of automobiles in shopping centers.

Your local newspapers will turn out to be invaluable for you. When you think about newspapers, though, don't limit yourself to the larger circulation dailies. Investigate small community newspapers. Larger cities in particular tend to have dozens of small papers that cater to those living within a certain geographical area. Someone interested in moving into that area is also apt to buy the paper for the classified advertisements that will list available apartments, used furniture for sale, or other services. This is a perfect place for your ad.

Some newspapers are supported solely by advertisers and are distributed free. These so-called pennysavers also are well read for their ads. Because these papers are used by local merchants, it is a good place for you to be seen. After all, you are interested in building up goodwill among local businesses, and what better way to do that than to advertise where they advertise?

Pennysavers also can be very efficient. In most markets, separate editions are printed with different merchants appearing in each. You can ask to be included only in the areas you wish to reach. This targeting will help you reduce waste and advertising costs.

With both local newspapers and pennysavers, you will have the choice of writing a classified ad, which will probably consist of two or more typed lines describing your service, or a display ad, which is larger and allows the use of graphics. You may want to use both. The advantage of the classified ad is that it is cheaper and can be run more frequently. But display ads are more likely to catch the eye of a potential customer. Also, you can use more creativity with a display ad, possibly illustrating your service rather than just describing it in print.

If you are unsure of the approach you should take, ask the advertising representatives at these papers for help. However, keep in mind that at many of these small operations, the same person who sells ads may also be the person who writes the editorials. If you sense you could get better advertising advice elsewhere, then do.

Be sure to look into other local publications. Church or synagogue bulletins often take advertisements. Large corporations or associations also have in-house newsletters that reach employees and members. Ads in these vehicles will be low cost.

To reach the largest number of people in your community, you will want to use one or more of your larger local newspapers. While the rates at these papers will be more than at the pennysavers, the cost will still be reasonable. Most local newspapers have rates to accommodate local merchants. You would not pay what a national advertiser like Procter & Gamble would pay.

One word of advice: When you use a local paper, insist on having your advertisement run where it will be seen by those readers who will be most interested in your service. If you are going after those about to tie the knot, try to get some assurance that your ad will appear on the same page or adjacent to the page that carries announcements of weddings, engagements, anniversaries, and other society events. If you are videotaping sports events, then you want your ad to run in the sports pages.

If you need it, ask for help in writing your ad, as most local newspapers will have someone experienced in advertising running the advertising sales department. In fact, it would be a good idea for you to introduce yourself to this person, so that he will become acquainted with you, your business, and your goals.

Whether you write the ad yourself or manage to get a professional to do the job for you, remember some basic principles. "It doesn't have to be full of fancy slogans," said Al Hampel, who has written advertising copy for General Foods, Johnson & Johnson, and Eastern Airlines. "The simpler, the better." Stress that your service is new, include a concise description of it, and state the value to the consumer. An example for a video dating service follows.

VIDEO DATING
THE NEW WAY TO MEET THAT
SPECIAL SOMEONE

*At Video-Mate, you can view the videotapes of other single profes-
sionals and we will introduce you to the ones you want to meet.*

*Don't waste another evening in a singles bar. Visit our convenient
midtown location today.*

VIDEO-MATE, INC.

1000 MAIN STREET

ANYTOWN, U.S.A.

555-666-7777

Probably one of the best places for your ad to be seen is in
the Yellow Pages. More than one video entrepreneur interviewed for this book claimed that a great percentage of his
business came from being in the Yellow Pages. In fact, one
videographer said that his business had been hurt because he
had neglected to check into closing dates for Yellow Pages
advertising and therefore missed the deadline.

The Yellow Pages are effective simply because people
who look through them are definitely in need of a service. If
someone looks at your ad under "Video," it is because he is
looking for someone to videotape something for him. In addition, the Yellow Pages' rates can fit into your budget because the editions are localized, allowing you to purchase
just the editions you want. You may want to have your ad
included under several different listings. If you are running a
wedding video service, your ad could run under "Video" and
under "Weddings."

Magazines are another print medium worth investigat-
ing. A magazine can be particularly useful if the people you
are trying to reach make up that magazine's audience. If you

are selling a video legal service, for example, advertising in special interest publications for lawyers would be a sure bet. Any of the regional or city magazines would be perfect for advertising a video dating service.

Don't dismiss a national magazine because you fear the advertising rates may be too high. Many of these magazines have regional editions where rates are lower. In addition, many have classified sections in the back where your ad could run at low cost.

When TV came on the scene, many people were predicting the end of radio. Instead, radio has emerged stronger than ever. While people may watch TV, they still listen to radio—in the car, while bustling around their apartments, even while rollerskating and jogging, thanks to headphones. Your potential customers are out there listening. Radio is the perfect medium for your business.

Part of radio's attraction is that you can target your audience. Advertising a video legal service? Then advertise on an all-news radio station. Video dating? Get your commercial on a rock station. Weddings? Rock again, or perhaps Country and Western or easy listening.

Radio also is attractive because it is economical. Ads on local radio stations are very reasonable, considering the number of people you will be reaching.

Don't think you have to come up with a fancy jingle. Of course, that would be great if you have the time and talent. But a well-written spoken ad will be just as effective. When composing your ad remember to keep it short and sweet. Emphasize the main points of your business so that those points will stick in the listener's mind. Also be sure to repeat your name, location, and phone number at the end of the commercial.

It seems such a natural. You are selling a video service, so what better place to advertise than on TV? Don't assume that the cost is too high. Obviously, you cannot afford a one-minute spot during a prime-time network show. But TV today is much more than the networks. There are many other opportunities open to you.

A great many of the commercials you see on television are not national anyway. Local stations sell air time too, and their rates are lower because the commercials will reach a smaller local audience instead of a huge national one. There are also bargains to be found during fringe times, early morning and late night. Just tune in at 3:30 A.M. and you will see many commercials for local merchants.

Your immediate reaction might be, who will see my ad in the middle of the night? Data on off-hour viewing is sketchy, but no one doubts the fact that there are many people tuning in to television at odd hours of the day. Witness all the 24-hour cable channels and the late night/early morning news shows started by the three major TV networks.

In addition to local broadcast TV, you will want to look into cable. Advertising costs on cable are very reasonable, often a fraction of what you would pay on broadcast TV. There are some excellent cable channels now in operation. As with broadcast TV, most of these cable services allow for the sale of local advertisements which are sold by individual cable systems. A good way to start making inquiries would be to call the cable system you or your neighbors subscribe to, or the one nearest you if your area does not have cable yet.

What should your ad on TV look like? As with print and radio advertising, your best approach would be to keep it simple. "Forget about the commercials you've seen on TV and get a good talking head on camera," advised Al Hampel. Don't think you can't produce an attractive, effective commercial at low cost. "I have seen some cable commercials produced for $5,000 that are more effective than commercials produced for $500,000," said Al.

Even if your video business does not produce commercials, it would not be difficult for you to shoot a simple commercial using your own equipment. Or it might be possible for you to find a colleague who has had some experience producing commercials and would do yours inexpensively. This might be another barter situation. Someone connected with a cable system might also lend his expertise to help you produce the commercial. After all, they have the equipment, and they are eager to sell the commercial time.

Whatever you do, be sure to ride herd on your advertising plan. Constantly assess your progress. Try to determine how each medium is working for you. Be sure to view each of your TV commercials when it is shown. Call the station if there is a problem. Check each of your print advertisements after it appears to make sure that it ran correctly and that it was not "buried." If there was a mistake in the ad, report it immediately. Most publications will run the ad again free of charge. If you find your ad was hidden, make sure to register a complaint and ask to have the ad rerun.

Also police any posters you have left in stores or on bulletin boards. Make sure they are still intact and clean. If you had attached tear-off cards, make sure there are some left. In addition, use these checkups as a chance to renew your acquaintance with each local merchant whose hospitality you are enjoying. Remember, you are counting on his recommendation to his customers, so a visit now and then will remind him you are still in business.

What if you are marketing a service that must be sold to professionals? How do you convince these people?

Al Hampel suggests that you send these sales prospects a well-written letter telling them about your service. But he continues that you should not stop at the written word but use video to illustrate the advantages of your service. "I bet there isn't a prospect around who wouldn't sit still for a video demonstration that could show him how he could better do his job," he said.

If you are trying to interest real estate agents, for example, why not make a videotape in which you ask people who are selling or buying homes how they would feel about using a video real estate service? In a two- or three-minute tape you could make quite a case for such a service. Picture an interview with a harried customer who has just spent an entire day viewing only five homes, all of which have been ruled out. It is a hot day, the traffic was heavy, and the customer's disheveled appearance reveals the ordeal he has been through. When you ask this customer how he would feel about shopping for a new home through video, he responds enthusiastically. What real estate agent interested in increasing business would not pause to think about adding such a video service?

You may not be able to afford to have John McEnroe endorse your service, but you may have less famous satisfied customers who might be willing to help you with publicity. "When I'm satisfied, I'm very eager to pass that on to others looking for a similar service," said Al Hampel.

The best way to use customer endorsements is as references. If you have videotaped someone's personal belongings and he was pleased with the job, ask him if you may give his name to others as a recommendation. Many potential customers may be helped to make up their minds after hearing a former customer praise your work. It also will help reassure those customers who are concerned about security. After all, when you hire someone to come in and videotape your possessions, it's necessary to trust that person.

If it happens that someone well known in your community, or famous on a larger scale, uses your service and is satisfied, don't hesitate to ask whether you can use his name in your advertisements.

Because there is so much interest in video, many of the new businesses being launched are receiving a great deal of publicity because they are new and different. This is the best kind of advertising you can get. It's free, oftentimes the stories are well placed and include photographs, and one write-up usually is followed by another since many news organizations get ideas for stories from each other.

How do you cash in on this bonanza? Don't assume that local news organizations are going to discover your business on their own. They just might, but don't count on it. You will have to do a little advance work for yourself.

Select those newspapers, magazines, TV shows, or whatever where you would love to be mentioned. Don't be afraid to aim high. Joan Hendrickson was determined to talk about her video dating service, the Georgetown Connection, on "The Phil Donahue Show" and on the front page of the *Wall Street Journal*. And she managed both feats. How? She was persistent and aggressive. She wouldn't take no for an answer, even after many rejection letters from the Donahue producer.

Joan was assertive because she knew her story was right for these two places. That point is crucial. Be familiar with the publications and TV shows you are trying to sell to. Pitch your story to them in a way that fits their editorial style. If it's a business publication, take a business approach. If it's a feature-type magazine, stress the human interest part of your business.

Address your letter to an individual. If you are writing to a newspaper, try to select a reporter or feature writer who you think would be interested in your story. If you are selling a video legal service, for example, telling your story to the legal affairs reporter would be a good place to start. When approaching a TV program, write to the producer.

Running a video business will require that you demonstrate many different skills. One of the most important will be your ability to sell. You may see yourself as a creative person who is too busy to think about advertising, but unless you can afford to hire a specialist to handle this area for you, then you will have to do the job yourself or your business will suffer. If you have a video idea that you really believe in, it will be easy for you to display the enthusiasm that will sell others on your idea.

5

How to Set Up Your Business

ONCE YOU have decided to launch a video business, you will be faced with many other decisions. At the top of the list will be how much money you will need. To a great extent the answer to that question will depend on how much money you can afford to invest. You don't want to pour your entire life savings into your business. You do want to invest enough to get the business off the ground, but you also want that amount to be something you can comfortably afford.

In coming up with that monetary figure, there will be other questions you will have to answer. Do you want to work out of your home or rent office space? Will you operate your business on a part-time or full-time basis? Can you afford to hire full-time help or will you use free-lancers? How much equipment should you buy? Should you specialize in one area, or generalize in order to maximize your business opportunities?

As you struggle to answer these questions, remember that in the beginning it is best to err on the conservative side. You can always move to rented quarters from your home. But it will be more difficult to move back home once you have signed a lease for space in an office building. If you are unsure about whether you can earn a living through video, then it is wise to start out working on your business part time without jeopardizing your other job.

Rather than burden your new business by paying salaries to other people, it would be better to use free-lancers when you need them. Even when you set out to buy equipment, the experts advise buying less than you think you need. It is always possible to add other components but more difficult to get your investment back on used equipment.

Unless your research has shown beyond a shadow of a doubt that there is enough business in a given area for you to specialize, begin by taking a variety of video assignments. "If you specialize, you're going to be passing up a lot of business," said Steve Sarabande, general manager of Famavision and Fama II Productions in New York. You will get valuable experience by hopping from one job to another. Many video people continue to handle anything that comes their way. Others, after a period of time, find one area more appealing. By keeping an open mind, you may discover a part of video that you never even considered.

Before you make any decisions, it is best to consult an accountant. There have been some major changes in the tax laws during the past few years. You want to find out how these laws will affect you. An accountant, especially one that specializes in helping small businesses, will be invaluable to your future. In setting up your business, you will be faced with many choices. No two situations are exactly alike. Your accountant can steer you on the course that is best for you.

Once you have established a good relationship with your accountant, you will be able to consult with him from time to time as problems come up. He will become knowledgeable about your business and will certainly earn his fees in what he saves you in taxes and other costs.

Of course, don't expect your accountant to do all the work. It is your business and your accountant will expect you to have done your homework before you come to see him. He can help you determine how much money you will need to start your business. But first you should get a pencil and paper and work out your own estimate. Table 1, which is based on information from the Small Business Administration, can help you work out these numbers.

Begin by putting in column 1 your estimated monthly expenses for things like rent, advertising, telephone, and insurance. Then using the formula given in column 2, multiply that amount and place the resulting figure in column 3. The bottom half of the chart includes one-time expenses for equipment, inventory, and other items. Most of these estimates will be made after you have consulted outside sources. For example, you will have to check with your local utilities to see how much money you will need for deposits. Once you have gathered these figures, place them in column 3.

Now, add up all the items in column 3 and you will arrive at the total estimated cash you will need to start your business. If that amount exceeds what you planned to spend, then you will have to make some adjustments, perhaps working out of your home or cutting back on your equipment purchases. If the amount greatly surpasses what you can afford to spend, then you should do some serious rethinking about launching your business. Undercapitalization is a prime reason new businesses fail. If you go in short on cash, you will be fighting an uphill battle.

You may want to consider borrowing money, but be warned that financial institutions are extremely choosy about whom they lend money to. They have to be. They are in business, too. You must demonstrate to a loan officer that your business is credit worthy, or you will probably be turned down. Banks like to make loans to companies that are growing and profitable. Unless you already are making money, it may be impossible to prove that you eventually will.

Even if you are accepted, it is more than likely that the

TABLE 1: Estimated Cash Needed to Start Your Video Business

Item	Column 1	Column 2	Column 3
	Estimate of monthly expenses	What to put in column 3	Estimate of cash needed to start business
Monthly expenses *(Enter in column 1)*:			
Salary of owner	_____	2 × column 1	_____
Other salaries	_____	3 × column 1	_____
Rent	_____	3 × column 1	_____
Advertising	_____	3 × column 1	_____
Delivery expense	_____	3 × column 1	_____
Supplies	_____	3 × column 1	_____
Telephone	_____	3 × column 1	_____
Other utilities	_____	3 × column 1	_____
Insurance	_____	Payment required by insurance company	_____
Taxes, including Social Security	_____	4 × column 1	_____
Interest	_____	3 × column 1	_____
Maintenance	_____	3 × column 1	_____
Legal and other professional fees	_____	3 × column 1	_____
Miscellaneous	_____	3 × column 1	_____
Starting costs you have to pay only once *(Enter directly in column 3)*:			
Fixtures and equipment			_____
Decorating and remodeling			_____

Item	Column 1	Column 2	Column 3
Starting inventory			_____
Deposits with public utilities			_____
Licenses and permits			_____
Accounts receivable (What you need to buy more stock until credit customers pay)			_____
Cash (For unexpected expenses or losses)			_____
Other			_____
Total estimated cash you need to start (Add up all the figures in column 3)			$_____

bank or lending institution will attach certain conditions to your loan that could affect the way you operate your business.

You may have many reasons for launching your own video business. You want the independence of being your own boss. You want the opportunity to express yourself visually. You hope to make a name for yourself in the video world. But never lose sight of your major objective: making money. Unless you have a trust fund and can afford to dabble in video, you will have to support yourself with your new business.

The Internal Revenue Service defines a business as an activity carried on for livelihood or for profit. An activity is considered by the IRS to be engaged in for profit if it produces a profit in any two out of five years. Naturally, you hope to make a profit in five out of five years. To do so, you need to develop the right attitude at the beginning. There are many people who are in business for themselves, yet they are lucky if they break even. Why? Each of these people does not treat his business like a business.

You are not running a charity. Do not give your work away. Sure, you may have to do some free jobs in the beginning to get started. But don't make it a habit. It is difficult to say no to friends and relatives who expect you to come and videotape their parties and affairs for free. But there are only so many video jobs you can do in a week. If you are giving half your time away, how will you ever make money?

Some video people have learned this lesson the hard way. "I used to be so kind and I got ripped off very easily," said Carol Slatkin, co-owner of Spectra Video Services in Washington, D.C. "Now I can't be so easily taken advantage of. People have to understand video is an expensive business. The equipment costs a lot and you have to justify it. It's like renting a car. A car costs a lot, so you have to pay a certain daily rate to rent it."

With every job that you take on, ask yourself what your profit will be. Often a video person will take on a job he knows will be unprofitable because he needs the work or it appeals to him creatively. Resist the temptation to do that too often.

Follow the example set by Skip Winitsky, owner of Media/Arts Management Associates in Washington. Skip said his company drew up a proposal to make a videotape for a Washington-based association. The group loved the idea, but balked at the price tag. Skip's company refused to lower its estimate because Skip knew that he would lose money if he did. The association hired another video company to execute Skip's idea at less than half Skip's estimated cost. "I'm sure that company is having a problem trying to do our idea at the new price," said Skip.

Take steps to ensure that your customers pay promptly. When you contract for a video job, your customer should be required to pay you a certain percentage of the total cost. In most cases, this percentage should be 50 percent, with the balance due upon completion of the videotape. When your customer comes to collect the finished tape, he should pay you what he owes before you let him leave with the videotape.

This approach may sound mercenary, but it is necessary. Once your customer has left your office with your work, what incentive does he have to pay you? Even if he does eventually pay, you don't want to wait several weeks or months before receiving your money. After all, you paid for the equipment and labor and you need to cover those costs right away. It may not seem like much to let one customer pay later, but add many customers to that list and it soon becomes apparent that you will have a cash flow problem. How will you afford to take on other jobs if you are waiting for past customers to settle their accounts?

The smart video person will not alter this policy for anyone. One videographer reported that he once waived the down payment for a civic group whose reputation he trusted. Unfortunately, the official from this company who hired the videographer was not as trustworthy, and it was six months before the payment was made. And to get his money, the videographer had to chase his client around town.

What all this gets down to is thinking of your activity as a business. One exercise that will help you in that regard is record-keeping. When you tabulate your expenses and income every month and actually see your profit or loss, it may encourage you to tighten your belt.

Record-keeping, of course, is not optional. And it doesn't mean throwing receipts into your bureau drawer. You *must* keep good, accurate records for tax purposes. This record-keeping should begin on day one. After your business opens, you may be too busy with other details to think about setting up a bookkeeping system. Again, this is an area where your accountant can help. He can show you how to set up your books and how to manage them each month.

There are two types of bookkeeping systems—single-entry and double-entry. Single-entry is easier to handle, but double-entry has built-in checks so you can be sure of your accuracy. In general, single-entry bookkeeping is based on the income statement and not on the balance sheet. You would record your income and expenses through the daily summary of cash receipts, a monthly summary of receipts, and a monthly summary of disbursements.

Double-entry bookkeeping employs journals and ledgers. You would first enter transactions into the journal, and then record summary totals of those transactions into the ledger, usually on a monthly basis. This system is self-balancing since every journal entry is made up of both debits and credits. The sum of the debits must equal the sum of the credits. Eventually when everything is recorded in the ledger, the debits and credits totals would be equal, thus ensuring that the account balances.

You probably will want to check on the financial health of your business on a monthly basis. You can do this by drawing up a monthly balance sheet breaking down your assets and liabilities. Table 2 can assist you in this task.

You also will want to periodically prepare a profit and loss statement. A P and L statement, as it is called, will tell you whether your business made a profit or a loss during a certain time period. What should go into a P and L statement is shown in Table 3.

A P and L statement is a good way to assess what you are doing wrong. If your net profit is nonexistent or too low, then you need to make some adjustments. Are you paying out too much money in payroll or rent? Is your service being priced too low? Should you be buying your supplies in bulk to take advantage of discounts? Based on your findings, you should plan on making some adjustments. Your next P and L statement should show improvement.

Open a separate bank account for your business. In order to have a record of all payments, you should pay your business expenses by check. Avoid writing checks to "cash," because later it will be difficult for you to ascertain what those checks were for.

To take care of small items, you should set up a petty cash fund. This fund can be used to pay for items that are not covered by regular invoices. These items would include postage, cab or bus fare, and photocopying. Cash a check for about $25 and place that money in a box or drawer. Whenever money is taken out, it should be recorded on a piece of paper inside the box. When the fund is gone, the items should be tallied up. At any one time, the items listed plus the leftover cash in the drawer should equal the amount of the fund.

TABLE 2: Current Balance Sheet

ASSETS

Current assets:

Cash:

Cash in bank $_____

Petty cash $_____

Accounts receivable,
less allowance for
doubtful accounts $_____

Merchandise
inventories $_____

Total current assets $_____

Fixed assets:

Land $_____

Buildings $_____

Equipment $_____

Furniture and
fixtures, less
allowance for
depreciation $_____

Leasehold
improvements, less
amortization $_____

Total fixed assets $_____

Total assets (total current assets plus total fixed assets) $_____

LIABILITIES AND CAPITAL

Liabilities:

    Current liabilities:

        Accounts payable $_____

        Notes payable,
        due within
        one year $_____

        Payroll taxes and
        withheld taxes $_____

        Sales taxes $_____

    Notes payable, due
    after one year $_____

Total liabilities $_____

Capital:

    Proprietor's capital,
    beginning of
    period $_____

    Net profit for the
    period, less
    proprietor's
    drawings $_____

Capital, end of period $_____

Total liabilities and capital $_____

TABLE 3: Profit and Loss Statement

Gross sales $_____

Cost of sales:

    Opening inventory $_____
    Purchases $_____

    Total $_____
    Less ending inventory $_____

Total cost of sales $_____

Gross profit (gross sales less total cost of sales) $_____

Operating expenses:

    Payroll (excluding owner) $_____
    Rent $_____
    Payroll taxes $_____
    Interest $_____
    Depreciation $_____
    Telephone $_____
    Equipment/supplies $_____
    Insurance $_____
    Miscellaneous $_____

Total operating expenses $_____

Net profit (excluding owner's salary) $_____

Many of your expenses will be tax-deductible, so be sure to keep track of these by retaining the receipts. What things are tax-deductible? In general, expenses that can be considered legitimate business expenses can be deducted. Rent, for example, can be deducted only if it is for property that you are using in your business. You may be able to deduct part of the cost of your rent if you are working out of your home, but you should be careful here. These IRS rules have been changed, and you will want to check with your accountant to make sure you are on solid ground before you take a deduction. You also may deduct certain business-related expenses for travel, entertainment, or gifts. Again, it is a good idea to check these details with your accountant.

All the initial expenses that you had when you started up the business are treated as capital expenditures. They are a part of your basis in the business and not tax-deductible, according to the IRS. Expenses that were for particular assets, such as equipment, can be recovered through depreciation deductions. Certain start-up expenses and organizational expenses can be amortized—deducted in equal amounts over a period of sixty months or more. But you probably will be unable to recover other expenses until you sell or go out of business.

There are three forms of business: a sole proprietorship, a partnership, or a corporation. At some point, you will have to decide which form you want your business to be.

Your decision is not irrevocable. You may start out as a sole proprietorship and later decide to take on a partner or to incorporate.

A sole proprietorship is the simplest form your business can take. You and the business are inextricably linked. You *are* the business. Its liabilities become your own liabilities.

Most entrepreneurs do little thinking about this aspect of their business. As a result, many small video ventures are sole proprietorships, simply because the owner never considered the alternatives. Don't wind up a sole proprietorship by default. Do some research and be sure it is the best arrangement for you. If not, look into the other two forms.

There may come a time when you will decide you want to take on a partner. The IRS defines a partnership as the relationship existing between two or more persons who join together to carry on trade or business. Each partner, depending upon the agreement, would share in the profits and losses of the company.

If there is someone you are thinking about setting up a partnership with, there are important facts to consider. Be sure that you both share the same goals for your company. For example, you may want to take on all video jobs while your partner wants to specialize. Such a difference in outlook means you will run into problems later on. The best partner is one whose own talents complement yours. If you both are excellent cameramen, but lousy at business details, then it may not be the perfect marriage.

Working with a good friend or relative can sometimes be a mistake. Emotions can get in the way of what should be a business deal. You may enter into one of these partnerships for all the wrong reasons. Cousin Danny needs a job. Or your best friend Matilda thinks video would be fun. When you take on someone who brings nothing to the table but his relationship with you, there is bound to be trouble. No matter how hard you try, you will wind up feeling bitter about carrying this person.

The best partnerships are those that evolve out of a common need. One video person in Washington free-lanced and worked with another free-lancer whose work she admired. It turned out that he also wanted to open a video business, so they joined forces and launched their company. This is the best possible situation. These two people had worked together and had had the opportunity to learn about each other's work style and talents.

Whether your business is a sole proprietorship or a partnership, you should think about incorporating. You incorporate your business by obtaining a charter from the state. Once you do that, the corporation is recognized as a separate legal entity with rights, privileges, and liabilities distinct from yours. Forming a corporation can help to protect some of your own personal assets in the event that you are sued. "I'm incorporated," said Skip Winitsky. "If disaster struck, they could sue a corporation that owns a typewriter."

Your first step will be to obtain a certificate of incorporation. Many states have a standard form that can be used by small businesses. This form can usually be obtained from the state official empowered to grant charters.

This document will require, first of all, the corporate name of your company. In general, the name you have chosen must not be similar to the name of any other corporation authorized to do business in the state. In addition, the name must not mislead the public—for example, your state may prohibit the use of certain words, such as "bank," "insurance," or "railroad" in your company name. (For more information on choosing a company name, see chapter 7.) You must state the purposes for which the corporation is being formed. Some states permit broad language while others want more specific details. You will be asked the length of time for which the corporation is being formed, a period of years or in perpetuity. Among other things, you will be asked for the names and addresses of incorporators, as well as the names and addresses of those who will serve as directors.

You may be able to handle incorporating your company on your own, but it is best to engage an attorney. For one thing, to complete the incorporation process, you must hold a stockholders' meeting during which the corporate bylaws are adopted and a board of directors elected. A qualified attorney can help to organize this meeting and handle all the necessary details.

A corporation is the legal structure that will house your company. But you also have to worry about choosing the right physical structure for your company. The decision may be made for you if you cannot afford to rent office space. Some people, however, have the funds to rent office space but still choose to work out of their homes. Whether you should depends upon your own needs.

It also depends upon your home. If you are living with your pet rattlesnake and Alaskan husky in a small efficiency apartment, then finding enough room for video equipment will be tough. You do want to make a favorable impression on the video clients who come to your office to view sample videotapes of your work. If they have to pick their way across a living room crammed with video supplies, they may lose some of their enthusiasm. Be aware that it takes a special personality to live and work in the same environment. Some people like to leave the office at the end of the day and go home to relax. Often it is impossible to enjoy a little recreational time if your video work is staring you in the face.

In deciding whether to locate your business in your home or in a separate office, there are certain things to consider. Is your location convenient? Will it be conducive to walk-in trade? Are you located in a safe part of town, not only for the protection of your customers, but also for yourself and your equipment? Check to make sure there won't be a zoning problem. Also, look into the cost of fire and crime insurance.

Ideally, you would like to hire a full-time staff to help you run your fledgling business. But such a proposition can be expensive. Especially at the beginning, your business may run in waves. One month, you will be inundated with work and the next nothing will come your way. "It's either feast or famine," remarked one video person.

You want to remain flexible. During the times when you are not busy, it will be difficult for you to pay your staff. It is a much better arrangement to think about hiring free-lance help whenever you need it.

How do you locate reliable free-lance people, especially on short notice? Most of them belong to one of the unions, so a quick check with one of the locals will probably turn up some good recommendations. Places that rent and sell video equipment keep lists of available free-lancers. You also should call other video companies that use part-timers.

In general, free-lancers are dependable, competent, and cooperative. Anyone making it as a free-lancer has to be. Word of his incompetence would spread quickly and he would find it tough to make a living. Most video companies use the same free-lancers repeatedly. You probably will find you do the same, especially when you find a talented person you like working with.

What are the drawbacks to using free-lancers? The situation is not as attractive as having your own staff, where you get to know each person's strong points and these people, in turn, learn about you and how you want your video business run. You do not have to review small details with them before each job. Unless you use a free-lancer regularly, he will probably need more guidance.

Also, full-time employees are apt to be more loyal. They want your video company to succeed so that they can keep their jobs. A free-lancer is less likely to display such loyalty, especially if he is hopping around from one video company to another. Even so, any free-lancer will be looking for more work, and so will try to do a good job with the hope that you will hire him again.

Whether you hire a full-time staff or use free-lancers, you will have to decide when to delegate authority to others. This is harder than it sounds. Some entrepreneurs never learn how to delegate and instead insist on handling every last detail themselves. While you always want to remain in control, you must learn how to relinquish certain duties to associates.

There are several reasons why delegating authority is so important. First, unless you possess superhuman powers, you will not have the stamina to do everything yourself. You must concentrate on the matters that are most important. Tasks that can easily be handled by your employees should be.

Second, granting authority to employees will improve staff morale. Nothing is more disheartening than to be ordered around like a robot. Think back to your own work experiences. You probably most enjoyed those jobs where you had some responsibility.

How much responsibility you give to subordinates will be up to you. To a great extent, it will depend on who these employees are and how much you trust their abilities and loyalties. You should take advantage of their talents.

Of course, delegating authority does not mean giving up control. You are still the one in charge. If the company fails, your employees can find other jobs, but you will lose your investment. For this reason, many entrepreneurs continue to maintain a watchful eye, particularly over all financial matters.

6

How to Buy Equipment

THE MOST expensive decision you will make in setting up your video business will be the selection of the video equipment you buy. Because it is such an important decision, it is worth spending your time before you spend your money.

You want to make sure that the gear you buy is perfectly suited to you and your needs. While others can supply you with information, don't depend on them to make the final decision. Only you can determine what you need, are comfortable with, and can afford. "The one who will make it is someone who has done his homework—what the market is, what investment it will take, *and* what equipment he will need," said Jeff Steier, vice-president of MPCS Video Industries Inc., which sells video merchandise to large and small companies.

Video equipment is constantly being improved upon by the manufacturers. "You'll get a piece of equipment and it will be the newest and a month later the manufacturers will come out with something better," said Fred Russo, a videographer in Easton, Connecticut. Because of these constant changes, this chapter will not attempt to tell you what specific video components you should buy. Such an exercise would prove futile. Most of the equipment mentioned would be out of date by the time you read this. What this chapter does intend to do is to give you some guidelines on how to select the equipment you will need based on the business you are setting up.

Video terminology will intimidate many. You walk into a video store and the salesman starts to spew out names that resemble alphabet soup—RCA TK-76B, JVC CP-5500U, Sony VO2860A. What is the difference between a JVC RM 50U and a JVC RM 60U? Within minutes, you are totally confused and feel as if you are in a foreign country where you don't speak the language.

Video *does* have its own language, and once you master the basics, it is not as difficult as it sounds. Just remember that all those numbers and letters are merely used by the manufacturers to distinguish one piece of equipment from another. After a while, you will be familiar enough with the equipment you use, or hope to add, that you also will use the abbreviations. But in the beginning, you should concern yourself more with the actual features of each piece rather than in learning its code name.

Make an effort to educate yourself about video equipment before you go shopping. In doing so, you should start with some basic facts. There are two types of video equipment—consumer and industrial. And within those two groups, there are other categories.

Consumer equipment uses ½-inch videotape. There are two consumer formats: Betamax, which was developed by Sony, and VHS (for video home system), developed by JVC (the Japan Victor Corporation, owned by Matsushita, known in the United States as Panasonic). Although both of these systems utilize ½-inch tape, they are incompatible. The main difference is in the manner in which the videotape travels inside the cassette, from one reel across the capstan (the small cylindrical pulley that regulates the speed of the tape) onto the other reel. Sony's Betamax system uses U-loading, while JVC's VHS uses M-loading. In each case, the route traveled by the videotape inside the cassette resembles its letter.

Why are there two different consumer formats? The ego of the manufacturers. Each company believes its system is better and should be the standard. In fact, after Sony introduced its Betamax system, VHS was only one of several different systems to come on the market as competitors. The others are no longer around. JVC backed its VHS format with a solid advertising campaign and was able to carve out for itself a chunk of the market.

Other manufacturers now pay Sony and JVC for the right to market video equipment under their own trade names. Brands that use the Betamax format include Toshiba, Sears, Zenith, NEC, and Sanyo. Those that use VHS are Hitachi, Sylvania, Quasar, RCA, GE, Sharp, and Magnavox. VHS equipment and blank videotapes tend to be lower priced than those of Betamax.

The home systems are incompatible with industrial systems, which generally use ¾-inch tape. While the consumer ½-inch tape is more compact, ¾-inch is broadcast quality and is preferred by many professionals. There is an industrial ½-inch videotape, but that also is incompatible with the ½-inch consumer videotape. The hardware for this videotape is more sophisticated than the consumer versions, and more expensive.

There have been some improvements in the industrial ½-inch videotape, but most professionals still prefer the ¾-inch. Generally, the wider the videotape, the better the quality. Many TV stations, in fact, use 1-inch videotape. For your own purposes, you want to start with a master videotape that is of the highest possible quality. The reason is that once you start making copies, each copy will lose a little color and sharpness when compared to the original.

Manufacturers have begun marketing a high quality ¼-inch videotape, which many videographers feel could revolutionize the industry. "Quarter-inch tape has a definite advantage in that it can be carried around in a smaller cassette," said Jeff Steier.

Many video people, in fact, are holding off purchasing additional equipment until they can evaluate the ¼-inch equipment and videotape. Should you be concerned about this development? Is this a good time for you to buy? If you need the equipment now, then you may not be able to wait. There are already many VCRs out there and not everyone will rush out to trade in their ½-inch or ¾-inch model for a ¼-inch one.

Also, keep in mind that it is possible to transfer a recording from one size videotape to another, or from one format to another in the case of Betamax and VHS. This is an important point if you expect to work in ¾-inch but have some clients who want ½-inch videotapes. What you need to do the job is a VCR for the videotape you shot and a VCR in the new desired format, plus connecting cables for audio and video. You would simply play the videotape on the first machine and record it on the second.

You might be swayed in your decision on whether to buy industrial or consumer equipment not only by the quality of the ¾-inch videotape, but also by the durability of industrial hardware. The consumer VCR is designed for light use. The average consumer may use the machine several times a week to record programming, but you could be using your equipment eight hours a day every day.

Another fact to note is that the consumer equipment often will carry only a ninety-day labor and parts warranty, while the industrial equipment could include service for up to a year. Not only do you want to avoid unnecessary repair bills, but you also want to have equipment you can depend on. Constant breakdowns can hurt your business.

In fact, reliability of the equipment should be one of your major concerns. "Part of the reason the Japanese equipment has such a good reputation is that you can take it out of the box, plug it in, and it works," said Eugene Marlow, president of Media Enterprises Inc. Gene suggested that once you have narrowed down your choices you should check with video people actually using those models to find out what their experiences have been.

Reliability also extends to servicing. "A major thing to consider is the follow-through—how fast you can get parts, whether the manufacturer will make good on his equipment, and what it will cost," said Gene. For this reason, many video people tend to stick with major manufacturers and buy the equipment through an authorized dealer who provides servicing.

Before you set foot in your first video store, read up on the equipment that you are interested in. Get an idea of what is on the market. There are now several video magazines that include regular evaluations of video equipment. Study newspaper advertisements. Look at catalogs. Write to manufacturers for more information. Talk to as many video professionals as possible.

The ideal situation would be to try out the equipment you are considering before you commit your cash. Some video dealers will allow you to test out the equipment briefly in the showroom, but to really decide what the merchandise is like, you might consider renting it for a day. While this alternative may cost you some money, it could prevent you from making a major mistake.

Some manufacturers offer training courses where you can have a chance to use their products. Sony, for example, has a well-organized program called Sony Video Utilization Services, which provides training for the experienced video person as well as the novice. The Sony plan includes both studio and field work. A great advantage is that all the equipment used is state-of-the-art. These classes are held all over the United States as well as at the Sony Video Center on the campus of the American Film Institute in Los Angeles. Check with a Sony dealer in your area for more information.

You might even consider taking a quick video course at a local college or other school to acquaint yourself with the mechanics and terminology of video. Even if the equipment used is out of date (it probably will be, because colleges find it financially difficult to keep up with the latest), it will at least allow you some hands-on experience. A class also will provide you with other sources of information since your instructor or other students may have some advice about what equipment to buy.

Take careful notes on what you learn, in and out of class. These notes will come in handy when you finally go shopping.

Where will you buy your video equipment? Ever since consumer video equipment was introduced, video stores have been opening as fast as umbrellas in a rainstorm. In New York City it seems there is a video store on every block. Some of these stores specialize in renting and selling prerecorded videocassettes. Others also sell video equipment.

Many of these operations are franchises. Someone paid a fee to a large company for the right to own and operate one of the company's stores. But many in the video industry question the manner in which these stores have been set up. Often, the owners, managers, and employees have received minimal training. Their total knowledge about a piece of video equipment might consist of what they read out of the manufacturer's brochure.

They are going to be most interested in selling the equipment they already have in stock, even if that means that you end up with something that's out of date or not exactly right for your purposes. You want to avoid any high pressure in buying your video equipment. You can sense when you are being railroaded. Don't stand for it.

Also, don't be quick to go for the cheapest deal. Many of the video stores will be glad to beat the competition for a few dollars if it means they make the sale. And there are many operations that make no bones about the fact that they sell at the lowest price, but that all you get for that is the equipment—no help in selecting your gear, no servicing, and certainly no assistance later on when you run into problems.

If you really know what you are doing and do not expect to ask the store for advice, then by all means pay the lowest price. But keep in mind that you get what you pay for. Don't expect someone to hold your hand later on.

Ideally, what you are looking for is a video dealership that is not partial to any one brand of video equipment and that employs knowledgeable salespeople who can help you make decisions about what to buy. You also want a store that will service your equipment for a certain amount of time, offer you assistance in operating the equipment when you run into trouble (that means giving advice over the phone when you hit a snag in the middle of a shoot), and give you a good deal when you want to upgrade. Also, you want a place that will rent equipment to you—possibly on short notice—when you contract for a job and need something that you don't own.

To find such a video dealer you are going to have to shop around. You will probably find you have better luck at places that cater to a professional video crowd rather than to the consumer who walks in off the street. Ask video people you know where they bought their gear. If a video person does recommend a video store, ask him if you can use his name when you shop there. It may help to get you better service. Notice any retail stores mentioned in trade magazine articles, especially if the article quotes a specific individual. He might be someone you will want to contact.

If a local college, high school, YMCA, or other group has a video program, find out from the instructor where his group buys its equipment. When you write to manufacturers, ask about authorized dealers. If you know what brand of equipment you will end up buying, it is a good idea to deal with an authorized dealer where you can count on repair work.

Before you decide where to buy, visit several video dealers. Choose a time of the day to visit when they won't be overrun with customers. Avoid lunch hours and from 4:00 P.M. until closing. It will be difficult for you to carry on a conversation with a salesperson when he is being besieged by other customers. In fact, the best approach is to call the store in advance and set up an appointment with a salesperson. This puts him on notice that you are serious about buying, and that you want his undivided attention.

When you arrive at the store and meet the salesperson, explain that you are setting up a video business. Without going into great detail, tell him a little about your business so that he will understand how you will use your video gear. Impress upon him the importance of what you are doing. It may not be important to him. You might represent just another sale. But it is your money that you are spending to launch this business, and you want to make sure you spend it wisely.

After you have introduced yourself, ask the salesperson about his own background. Has he ever worked with video equipment? (If he does have some experience, then he will be able to give you his own observations.) This may strike you as overstepping. After all, who are you to ask this man about his credentials? You are a paying customer, that's who, and if you are going to trust his opinion, then you have a right to find out if his opinion is worth anything. Remember that some of these salespeople are not well versed in the video area and may have been selling shoes last week. That is not the type of person you want to deal with.

If you are not satisfied with your salesperson's background, tell him politely, but firmly, that you would like to deal with someone who has had some experience. If he balks, seek out the manager. Keep in mind that there are many places to buy video equipment. Unless the manager presents you with a salesperson you can trust and feel comfortable with, take your business elsewhere.

When you find a qualified salesperson and he shows you equipment, don't be afraid to ask him questions. Stop him if he uses a term or abbreviation you don't understand. You may be reluctant to show your ignorance, but it will be far worse if you pretend to know more than you do. You will only become savvy about video equipment if you ask questions, take notes, and evaluate all your information.

Starting out, you will need several pieces of basic equipment: camera, recorder, player, and color monitor. If you plan to do field work—videotaping events outside a studio—then you will need portable equipment. Comfort is a consideration here. Even when a certain camera or portable recorder/player comes highly recommended, if it is uncomfortable for you to carry around for a long period of time, it is not for you.

In the beginning, experts advise that you buy less equipment than you need. You can always add pieces later. But you should have a long-range plan. Keeping that plan in mind, you should consider the flexibility of what you are buying. Is what you have selected compatible with other items you might want to add in the future? Also, you might want to choose pieces that can be used both inside and outside a studio, even if you don't expect any field work in the beginning. "If you are going to build a system, make sure that it fits into a large scheme," said Gene Marlow.

You may decide to hold off on buying editing equipment. But as you build up the business, it is something worth considering. Renting editing facilities is expensive. It also leaves you at the mercy of the people who own the editing machines. If you have a rush job, you may not be able to get it done on time. Clients may be reluctant to hire you if they know that any editing expenses you incur will be added to their bill. A big plus for buying editing equipment, or any equipment for that matter, is that it can be amortized for tax purposes over the time that it is used.

Some video cameras and recorders now include features that can add special effects to your finished videotape. These features allow you to dissolve from one scene to another, change the background color, or split the screen. Some video equipment even permits you to "write" letters over the videotape. If the equipment you select does not include these sophisticated features, you may want to purchase equipment later on that can produce these effects.

As you move along, you may find yourself accumulating other things. Lights, for example, have a great advantage in that they never become obsolete. And lights can be very important to a good shoot. "The quality is a hundred percent better with proper lighting," said John Fama, president of Famavision and Fama II Productions. "You can never have too much lighting and you can never own too many lights. Lighting never gets outdated. It's the one investment where you can get your money back."

That is not true for other pieces of video equipment. "In this industry, even when you're buying a piece of equipment, it's already six months obsolete," said Fama. His complaint is echoed by a chorus of other video professionals who worry about the cost of keeping their video equipment up to date. Lee Roy Kaminski, owner and president of KTV Consultants Inc., said that when he was heavily involved in the production business (he now does more training and post-production work), he was buying two complete video systems a year. "I've got a couple of $12,000 doorstops around," he said, laughing.

Some video people go so far as to accuse the video manufacturers of staggering improvements so that every year they can bring out new improved products to increase their sales. At least one retail dealer does not discount that premise. "The manufacturers will say, 'If we don't make new things, we're not going to sell new things,'" he said. "The manufacturers have to have a story to tell and that story has to be something new."

But equipment manufacturers defend the practice. "Video is still going through a rapid development stage and every new stage brings equipment with higher performance," said Robert Mueller, vice-president, Sony Video Communications. "The state of the art is advancing very quickly."

There is a division of opinion over whether you should concern yourself with every single change that the manufacturers introduce and what role the changing climate should have on your immediate purchasing decisions. A great deal will depend on your clients. Consumers are less likely to keep up to date on these improvements. On the other hand, business clients will be more knowledgeable. "If you spent five million dollars today, you would buy the latest state of the art," observed Jeff Steier of MPCS. "Three weeks later, if they came out with a machine that does one thing more, the advertising agencies would want you to use it."

Notwithstanding such demanding clients, Jeff does not

see much reason to upgrade equipment constantly. "There is no such thing as obsolete," he said. If the equipment still functions and does a good job, then use it, he said.

And most video people manage to use or rent out their older equipment. Lee Kaminski noted that one of his outdated cameras is still sought out because it can be used in the rain. John Fama observed: "I hold on to the stuff. I put it to use on something else."

Some video people avoid the whole problem of updating by renting instead of buying their equipment. There are several advantages to renting. Probably the most important is that you are always assured of getting the most up-to-date machines. Most places that rent will take the time to instruct you on operating any pieces that you are unfamiliar with. When you rent, you never have to worry about repairs and maintenance. In fact, many rental dealers will not charge you for equipment that doesn't work.

Renting relieves other headaches. You don't have to think about storing your gear, a factor if you are working out of a small apartment. You also don't have to worry about insuring it. There's no fear about equipment being stolen if you don't have any.

You can also satisfy individual client demands easier by renting. Especially if you deal with a rental place that stocks all the latest equipment, your clients will always be assured of getting exactly what they want.

The major drawback to renting is that it can be expensive. And even though the rented equipment can help you do a job, when you finish you walk away with nothing but the completed videotape. Most video people find that owning is better than renting, even owning outdated equipment.

You may want to compromise. You can begin by buying the basic equipment that you need. Whenever the situation calls for it, you can supplement your regular equipment with rentals.

By now you have grasped the point that equipment is a major investment. Any investment needs to be protected. Like all electronic equipment, video equipment can be sensitive. You may see TV newsmen rushing through crowds with their cameras knocking into everything in sight. You do not have the support of a TV station behind you, so protect what you own. Don't toss your video camera into a closet with the vacuum cleaner. Each component should be kept in its proper carrying case where it can be shielded from unnecessary bumps. Store all equipment at moderate temperatures.

Check your equipment every time you take it out of its case. When you notice something wrong, deal with it immediately. Unless you know something about repairs, avoid fixing equipment yourself. Take any equipment that is malfunctioning to a reputable repair place.

Video people have different attitudes about their equipment. Some, particularly those who specialize in video dating or video legal services, see it as a necessary evil. These people are more interested in the substance of their jobs and see the video equipment merely as tools to help them get those jobs done.

Others, however, regard good equipment as making up the core of their business, the underlying reason for their success. They lavish time and money on the care and feeding of cameras, recorders, lights. "Any money I make gets reinvested," said John Fama. "If I made a half-million tomorrow, I know exactly what I want to buy."

No matter which group you fall into, good equipment will be essential to the success of your business. Your purchasing decisions will be important ones. So take the time to consider all the data carefully before you plunk down your credit card.

7

How to Protect
What You Produce

EVEN BEFORE you open the doors to your new video business, you should give some thought to protecting yourself legally. Video is similar to many other businesses that deal with the public. You should be insured in the event of a physical accident—someone tripping over a wire, for example. But video carries with it other risks. In most cases, you are being called upon to record events that will only happen once. If something goes wrong, your customers may be angry enough to sue.

What follows is a list of some legal problems your video business may encounter, with advice on how to handle them. Since each case is unique, however, it is a good idea for you to contact a local lawyer early on. Discuss your business with him, giving him some idea of the types of situations that could develop. He will perhaps recommend that you draw up a standard contract for clients to sign that will protect your rights. If a crisis does occur, your lawyer will have the background information necessary to handle your case.

It's difficult to think about paying a lawyer's fee when you have yet to make your first buck. But when you run into your first legal hassle, you will be glad you enlisted this professional.

You come up with a unique video business and know that you will be a success only if you can prevent others from stealing your idea. Can you keep others from copying it?

In short, no. There is no way for you to protect an idea with the traditional forms of protection, namely trademarks, patents, and copyrights. No one owns an idea. So if you dream up videotaped résumés, for example, there is no way to stop someone from opening up a similar business.

The best protection is to get there first. If you have your video résumé service up and running and earning a name for itself years before your competitors, you will have the edge.

You have been in business for more than a year. One day you notice a newspaper advertisement for a new video business with the same name as yours. Can you prevent this new company from using your name?

Maybe. If you really have been in business longer and can prove it by supplying dated proof of when you made your first sale, you may be able to convince the offending party to change his name. If he won't change his name voluntarily, you will have no choice but to bring legal action, charging him with trademark infringement.

Before you get into a legal dispute over your name, do some serious thinking about what you want to call your company.

There is no doubt that a catchy name will bring in business. If someone is thumbing through the Yellow Pages he will be stopped by a well-written advertisement that includes an interesting name. But a well-chosen title also could help you avoid a trademark battle.

Your inclination will be to include the word "video" in your title. But think twice about doing so.

From a marketing point of view, having video in your company's name helps to get across immediately what your company does. Tacking on a second word (Legal, Weddings, Memories, Portraits) adds further explanation. In fact, a name like Video Weddings completely conveys your purpose to the customer.

So what's wrong with names like that?

For one thing, these names are hardly unique. Open up a phone book, particularly one in a large metropolitan area. Chances are you will run across dozens of companies with video in their names. After a while they all begin to sound alike. It's easy to imagine a customer confusing Video Date and Video Match.

A more important point is that you will have a difficult time protecting your company's name if it is so common and if it is too descriptive of the services you are offering. "You have limited protection when you register your mark in a crowded field," said Barbara Dill, an attorney and president of Barbara Dill & Associates, a New York–based legal consulting service. And you do want to protect your company's name. After all, you are sure your company will be a success. You want to continue to build on that reputation. You don't want other companies coming along using your name and benefiting from your hard work.

Trademark experts recommend selecting a name that is arbitrary. The most famous examples of such names include Xerox and Kodak. These names require more advertising because you really are starting at ground zero and have to explain to the public what the company does. Unless you have the advertising budget of a Xerox or Kodak, you probably will decide against such a name.

The best strategy is the middle ground, selecting a name that avoids the obvious, yet helps to convey a sense of your purpose. The Georgetown Connection, for example, while saying nothing about video in its title, gets across the idea that it is a vehicle for bringing people together. A potential client is attracted by that fact and then later learns Georgetown Connection is a video dating service.

The best procedure to follow is to select several names that you are considering for your company. Then for a small fee you can engage a trademark search firm (two of the best are Thomson & Thomson in Boston and TCR Service in Englewood, N.J.) to comb through the federal registry of trademarks to see whether anyone is already using that name.

The search firm will "cover the waterfront," according to attorney Dill, and present you with a whole list of names that might be similar to yours. In addition, the search firm will look for company names that are not in the federal registry but may be operating in your area and could prevent you from using your chosen name. If the search turns up any marks that are similar to any of the names you are considering for your new business, you should consult an attorney who can advise you whether it is safe to use them. Keep in mind that the search firm cannot guarantee it has located every last company whose name might be similar.

After you have all this information from the search firm, you can decide on a name. If you plan to register your trademark in Washington, you must have proof documenting when you first used that name in an interstate sale. The date of that sale will mark the first use of the trademark.

Don't go to sleep after your trademark is registered. Constantly be on the lookout for others using your name. If you are sure you were using your trademark first, a letter to the offending party with a copy of your federal registration should be enough to convince him. "If he's smart he'll back off," said Barbara Dill.

If you are operating a local business and do not plan to make any interstate sales, then it still is possible for you to register your mark on the state level. You should check with the appropriate state agency.

It is not necessary to register your company name in order to be protected. But if you do not register your mark, be sure to keep documented proof of your first interstate or intrastate sale. In the event someone contests your use of the name, you will be able to prove when you began using it.

You take a video deposition and, even though you checked your equipment thoroughly before beginning, something happens to the audio quality of your tape. Before the lawyers can arrange to take the deposition again, the witness dies. Can you be sued?

A well-written contract signed by your client before you start the job can help you escape liability in this situation. While such a contract would state your intention to deliver satisfactory work, this legal agreement also should include a disclaimer to cover you in case circumstances beyond your control prevent you from doing so. An equipment breakdown would fall into this category.

Just as a precaution, however, you might want to back up your video equipment with audio equipment. More than one legal videographer reports they often tape-record depositions simultaneously in the event something happens to the audio quality of the videotape. And if a mishap were to befall both the audio and video portions of the videotape, at least you would have the tape recording to give your client. Such a safeguard would also demonstrate your good intention to deliver satisfactory work.

*You agreed to videotape a wedding and thought you had talked
out all the details with the client. But when you deliver the tape,
he expresses disappointment with the job and threatens not
to pay. What do you do?*

If you do not have a signed contract, it will probably be impossible for you to force the client to pay.

If you are operating a consumer business, don't take it for granted that the client understands what you will deliver. Oral agreements always are chancy, but in video they are particularly so. You should work with your lawyer to devise a standard contract that each client can sign. This contract should be written in laymen's language and should be no more than a page long. Otherwise you are apt to scare off a client before you have even loaded your camera.

The customer's foremost concern is that you produce a videotape of good quality, so the contract should state that as your intention. The contract should state approximately how many hours of tape you will shoot and how long the final tape will be. If you plan to show the unedited tape to the client, thus giving him some say in what is included in the final tape, then the contract should say so. You will want to include a time limit for such feedback, however, so that the client doesn't hold up your work for weeks while he tries to decide which scenes he wants cut.

You also should include certain disclaimers in the event you are prevented from delivering satisfactory work. You are just as vulnerable to equipment breakdowns as a legal videographer and should cover yourself. You also want to avoid being held responsible in the event officials at the church, synagogue, or wherever you will be shooting prevent you from doing your job. The best way to accomplish this is to put the burden on the client, requiring him to make prior arrangements.

The contract also should be structured so that you can add provisions to it depending upon the job you are doing.

You show up to videotape a wedding and find out that the wedding has been called off. How can you be sure you will be compensated for your time even though you have not shot a single foot of tape?

Your contract should include provision for a "kill fee" so that you will be guaranteed payment even if the affair you were to tape never takes place. Such a provision should give the client an opportunity to notify you in advance without paying a penalty. You should decide how much notice is reasonable.

You videotape a backyard party and happen to catch one of the guests jumping into the pool without his clothes on. He later threatens to sue you unless you excise that portion from the tape.

Your contract should also include a "hold harmless" clause, which states that you will not be held liable for any legal action that may result from the videotape. Even if the star of the tape threatens to sue you, and the client tells you it's your problem, a signed contract with this provision will make it the client's problem.

Before you videotape a party, be sure to discuss with the client his expectations. Does he want you to videotape rowdy behavior on the part of his guests? This may be a wild and crazy bunch and the client may complain if your tape is too tame. Take your instructions from him—after he has signed the contract, of course.

If you do want to avoid problems with guests, Barbara Dill recommends making a loud announcement when your camera begins to roll, stating that you are videotaping the party and suggesting that anyone who is camera shy should move out of range.

You are in the business of videotaping entertainers. Five years ago you did a tape for someone who is now a big star. Do you have the right to sell that tape to others?

Yes, if the entertainer has signed a release giving you permission to use the tape for other purposes.

If you are in the business of videotaping performers, you should ask your lawyer about composing a standard release form for these clients to sign before you do the videotaping. It is possible to get a performer to sign a release afterward, but it may be more difficult to do so.

In general, such a form states that you are free to use that videotape at some future time. Releases vary greatly; some performers literally sign away all their rights when they agree to be photographed. You will have to decide what type of release will be comfortable for you and acceptable to your clients.

You invent a device to help you in your video business. Can your invention be protected?

You may apply for a patent for your device. Patents are obtained for a period of seventeen years and give you the right to stop others from making, using, and marketing your device.

Before you are granted a patent, however, you may have to prove to the U.S. Patent and Trademark Office that your device is new and useful, and that it would not have been obvious to a person of ordinary skill in the field. You will need to hire a law firm specializing in this field to conduct a search for you at the U.S. Patent and Trademark Office in Arlington, Va., and to prepare a patent application if your idea looks promising.

Applying for a patent can be time-consuming and expensive, and enforcing your patent after you obtain it can be costly. Also, when you obtain a patent, the details of your invention become available to the public. "It is better sometimes just to go out, make the device, and sell a whole lot of them before anyone figures out how you did it," said Anthony Hoffman of Cralin & Co.

One of your trusted employees leaves and, using your customer list, sets himself up in a competing business. Can you stop him?

Yes, as long as you have taken the proper precautions to protect yourself against theft of your trade secrets. These precautions should include advising your employees of their obligations not to disclose confidential business information to others outside your organization, and following that policy yourself.

You should let your employees know what information you regard as being confidential (lists of your customers, for example). Invest in a "confidential" stamp and use it on important documents not meant to be seen by the public. And you should keep your valuable business information in a safe place under lock and key.

If you have been casually handing out information regarding the identity of your customers and the tricks of your trade, it is unlikely that you will succeed in convincing a judge or jury that these are worthy of legal protection. Keep in mind, however, that usually you cannot prevent someone outside your organization from imitating unless you hold a patent.

*You complete a videotape and want to prevent anyone else
from copying it. Can you do so?*

You may copyright the tape. To register the copyright, you
must submit copies of your work to the Copyright Office in
Washington, D.C. However, even without a registered copyright, you are protected from the moment you create the
work. Registration is only necessary if you wish to sue someone for infringement of your copyright. And if that becomes
necessary, you can obtain a registration on short notice. It is a
good idea to place a copyright notice at the beginning of the
tape. The preferred form of notice would include the familiar ©, followed by your name or the name of your business,
and the year.

8

Video in
Show Business

MANY ENTREPRENEURS who want to make it in video hope to do so in the entertainment area. The attraction is easy to see. Entertainment video is glamorous. Video people working in Los Angeles and New York mingle with the big names in show business. The exposure can sometimes lead to a prestigious job with a TV network or a Hollywood production company. The work can be very lucrative, and there is always the possibility of striking it rich with a videotape that really takes off.

It's not surprising that entertainment video is one of the most competitive areas in which to launch a video career. More than any other segment of the video industry, *who* you know often counts as much as *what* you know. Those in entertainment video complain about back-stabbing, stealing of clients, and constant pressure to hold on to what they've built up. Yet many continue to work in entertainment video, and every year more people try to break into the industry.

If you aspire to a video career in entertainment, there are some things you should know.

First, be realistic. Don't expect to move to New York or Los Angeles and instantly set up a successful video production business. The competition is fierce. Most of the people in the field have trained elsewhere, "paid their dues," so to speak, by working for other video people. Along the way, they have met influential people in the industry and now have enough contacts to keep the jobs rolling in. It will take you a long time to build up similar contacts.

While your goal may be producing music video or other programs for cable TV, be aware that there are fringe areas of show business where it will be easier for you to get started. Increasingly, entertainers just starting out in the business are having their performances videotaped. These videotapes serve as a video résumé for these people when they audition. Such video jobs not only will give you valuable experience, but also will provide you with future contacts. Undoubtedly some of those people you videotape will make it and will remember you when they do.

In the entertainment area more than in any other, you cannot afford to fly by the seat of your pants. Entertainers, even those just beginning, are the most difficult customers to please. "Entertainers are the worst," said Steve Sarabande, general manager of Famavision and Fama II Productions. "It's the nature of the beast; it's a dog-eat-dog world." Added John Fama, president: "People are demanding of entertainers, and [when entertainers come to us] they are in the position to demand something from someone else."

A singer may not know anything about lighting, but she will know how she wants to look while singing in that darkened nightclub. It's up to you to know how to achieve that look. En route to the job is no time to be reading a manual on how to set up lights. If you don't have an experienced lighting person on board, then you should know how to light.

And lighting expertise is not the only talent you will need. Tapes for entertainers often are shot under stressful conditions. There is the audience to contend with. These people have paid to see a performance and can get nasty when their view is blocked by a video camera. You have to be good enough to continue to shoot even with interference.

Then there is the entertainer himself. More than likely he will be moving at a fast pace throughout his show and will expect you to catch his every move. You will have to follow him closely, possibly using several cameras and supervising your associates. The audio quality will be important, especially if you are taping a singer or band.

Finally, the whole thing must be skillfully edited to resemble an act straight from "The Tonight Show," because chances are that is where this performer would like to appear next.

All the talents you will need to compete successfully in entertainment video can be gained only through experience. But don't think you have to start at the top to get that experience. People who are making it in this area honed their talents by first doing other things in video. You may sniff at the idea, but videotaping weddings has been a valuable training ground for many of these people.

When you come right down to it, it's just as difficult to videotape a wedding in a dimly lit church as it is to tape a performer in a smoky cabaret. Instead of an audience, you have relatives and guests to contend with. Sound quality also is important. (You can't miss the bride whispering, "I do.") And some good editing can make even the dullest wedding look like the social event of the decade.

There also is the extreme pressure of knowing that if you blow the first take, you may never get a second chance.

But while the quality of those first few videotaped weddings may have been good enough to satisfy consumers, an entertainer will be quick to spot the flaws. And you can see the entertainer's point of view. She is looking to impress professionals such as directors and casting agents with her performance. If she doesn't look and sound her best, she will be out of a job and so will you.

While the entertainment world is competitive, there are still many opportunities for the video entrepreneur, especially those who are willing to start on a more modest level. Take a cue from those already working in the area. Many are reluctant to be totally dependent on this fickle industry. Therefore, these entrepreneurs continue to videotape weddings, bar mitzvahs, parties, and company conferences. You should do the same, at least in the beginning.

Don't assume you have to be in New York or Los Angeles. In fact, you may have a better chance of succeeding if you start in another city. While these other cities may not represent the major leagues, you will be getting valuable experience and have the videotapes to demonstrate what you can do. Later on if you want to get into the big time, these tapes will be your ticket.

Where should you look for clients? If you set up shop in Seattle or Cleveland, chances are you won't be videotaping Diana Ross or Michael Jackson. But remember, there are aspiring performers everywhere. One video entrepreneur approached a stand-up comic he found performing on the boardwalk in a resort town and convinced the entertainer he needed a videotape. Look around your own city, or wherever you happen to be. Chances are there are dozens of these street performers who are prospective clients.

Almost every city boasts its own collection of nightclubs, coffeehouses, and discos where young performers appear. It's a good bet that these performers have their sights set on making it in the big time, and videotapes of their performances will be the best ammunition they can have to impress those who can help their careers.

Make it a habit to skim the entertainment columns of

local newspapers and other publications. Before you approach a performer, take in his show so that you can say something positive. Be prepared to educate and sell these people on the advantages of having a performance videotaped.

What are the advantages? Videotapes are the best way to sell a TV act. Indeed, watching a videotape is like watching a TV show. After viewing a performer on videotape, a director or producer can judge whether his act will make it on TV.

If a performer really believes he is TV material, he should relish the idea of showing producers and directors what he can do. On a videotape, he really gets the chance to show his stuff. And because the videotape will later be edited, any gaffes, blunders, sour notes, or missteps can be removed. The producer will see the performer at his best.

A skilled videographer can make the performer look good. Even if the nightclub audience was half asleep, the video person can edit the tape to show only enthusiastic faces. If a long silence greeted the comic's best punchline, the videographer can add laughter.

Would-be performers should be easy to sell on videotaping for another reason. Videotape is rapidly becoming commonplace in the industry. Casting directors, agents, and others now expect to judge a performer by his videotapes. One casting director estimated that she views hundreds of videotapes each week to help her in her job of casting commercials, plays, and films.

"Anyone who has aspirations of making it in the entertainment business nowadays needs a portfolio and video will help him," said Steve Sarabande. Albert Dabah of Video Portfolios said many of the entertainers who come to him want videotapes made to get jobs on cruise ships. "Managers and agents want to see those tapes," he said. So a performer who relies on a printed résumé and still photographs is apt to be handicapped. The casting director will not have an inkling as to what the performer can really do.

Even models who get most of their income from appearing in printed advertisements and magazines are moving toward videotaped presentations to help them land TV jobs. Let's face it. TV jobs pay more and once most models have made it in print they naturally hope to make it on TV.

Video serves another function: It is the best way to preserve a good performance. Officials at New York City's Lincoln Center long ago realized video's potential. Lee Kaminski, now owner and president of KTV Consultants Inc., was called upon in the late 1960s and early 1970s to videotape ballets, operas, and plays at Lincoln Center. "Video is the perfect anthropological/archival tool," said Lee. "It disappears. It has no gears and makes no noise. People forget that it's there."

Lee said that many performers were suspicious of video in the beginning, but dancers were quick to appreciate this new medium. A singer has always had recordings. But a dancer has never before had a convenient, economical way to record for posterity what he or she could do at a certain point in a career. Video now makes that possible.

Although you will want to concentrate on contacting performers, don't overlook groups. Most communities have drama guilds that produce plays with local talent. High schools and colleges have drama and music departments that schedule regular productions. Some of these organizations may not have thought about videotaping their shows, but you can point out to them the value in doing so.

Colleges are perpetually in need of funds. Videotapes of drama productions could illustrate some of the marvelous activities the college offers students. Such a videotape could be used quite effectively not only in fund-raising campaigns but also in recruiting efforts.

Local TV stations always are looking for "filler," two- or three-minute segments that help to fill time at the end of a news broadcast. While one of these TV stations might not send a cameraman to videotape a local production, it just might find a spot to publicize the play if supplied with a videotape by the group. That plug no doubt would help the group increase its gate receipts.

The historical value of such videotapes is also important. Most school and community groups tend to produce the same plays or musicals in cycles. It would help this year's cast of *The Music Man* to see what was done by local talent five years ago.

Once you have videotaped an entire production, it's possible that individual cast members will ask for copies to keep themselves. If you have the facilities to produce extra tapes, this duplicating can help to bring in extra income.

Department stores in major cities have been using video effectively to help increase sales. Television sets are set up in various boutiques or departments throughout the store. While a customer is browsing through the Ralph Lauren boutique, for example, she can also view the designer's complete collection shown by models who have been videotaped.

Sometimes these videotapes are of the actual runway shows staged for the New York press. Other times these tapes have been produced for the designer or the department store. A customer may see an outfit on the videotape that is not in the store but could be ordered. Showing these tapes also creates an atmosphere of excitement about the clothes, which puts customers in the proper frame of mind to buy.

You may not have the opportunity to videotape Ralph Lauren, but there are probably department stores or boutiques in your area that sponsor fashion shows with local models and would like to show that videotape later in the store. Even if the store does not stage fashion shows, the manager might be receptive to purchasing a videotape that features clothes from his shop. Lee Kaminski made videotapes for one Madison Avenue boutique in New York that played them in the window to entice people to enter.

As you can see, there are many opportunities for entertainment video on the local level. Use your imagination to create other possibilities.

Even before your camera starts to roll, you and the performer should agree on what the final videotape will be. Albert Dabah of Video Portfolios reports that he has as many as three meetings with the performers to talk over the job. "It is important to find out what their expectations are," he said. Albert always offers to show the client some tapes to illustrate the possibilities.

The performer should decide whether he wants a simple one-camera shoot with no editing or a more elaborate shoot with two or more cameras, editing, and possibly special effects. Because of the price, many performers opt for the simple one-camera shoot.

Videotaping a performer can be done either in a studio or on location. Shooting in a studio allows a more controlled situation for both the performer and the videographer. You won't have to tote your expensive equipment crosstown in a cab. There is no interference from crowds or the audience. You don't have to get permission from the club owner to set up lights. You can shoot several takes of the performer's act and have him choose the one he likes best.

Of course, if you don't have studio facilities yourself, you will have to rent them, and in major cities that could be expensive. Keep in mind that in many cases, however, it might be possible for you to do the videotaping in your own home or office. Albert Dabah lives in a modest-sized New York apartment, but he has managed to carve out a space in his living room that he uses as a studio. He has suspended from his ceiling a backdrop that can be pulled down behind the performer. Often performers, especially those just starting out, feel more relaxed performing in someone's living room rather than in a large impersonal studio.

Of course for dancers, bands, and large groups, you will have no choice but to shoot in a studio or on location. There is a major advantage to shooting on location. The videotapes appear more lively when you have audience reaction and can capture how the performer and audience interact. This is especially important for a comedian, magician, or performer who feeds off the crowd's response. Such synergism will no doubt give the director or agent a positive feeling when he views the tape. And of course a videotape that shows the performer actually working in front of a live audience can only enhance his status as a professional and increase his chances of landing other jobs.

If you are planning to shoot on location, there are several things you should do. A visit to the club, restaurant, or other facility is a must. Check the available lighting and determine how much supplemental lighting you will need. Although the performer should be responsible for telling the club owner about the shoot, it is a good idea to double-check to make sure you have clearance. Even if the club owner has okayed a shoot, he might be opposed to the use of extra lights that will bother the audience. You should know these things beforehand.

Also check to see whether the club is covered by union contracts. If it is, and you are not a union member, then you will not be able to shoot there.

To ensure an ebullient crowd, remind the performer to invite friends and relatives to the club on the night of his taping. Have these fans sit up front where you will easily be able to capture some of their faces.

If the club manager objects to videotaping during customer hours, then perhaps you can arrange to use the club during the day. The performer could pack the house with his friends and relatives and you would be able to videotape unimpeded.

Most videographers expect the performer to have a good idea of what he will do on the tape. The executives at Famavision and Fama II Productions hold several preproduction meetings with the client to hammer down all the details. And Albert Dabah of Video Portfolios is not bashful about throwing in his own suggestions. Albert was an actor once himself and so knows something about working in front of the camera as well as behind it. If he feels the actor is foundering, he will help.

How much time you spend with the performer before you shoot is up to you. But if you are interested in making a good tape to please this client, thus ensuring his return and his recommendation of your service to other actor friends, then some extra rehearsal time is a good idea. Albert Dabah finds that most actors need to be helped to find the right voice level for video. Stage actors in particular are used to projecting their voices to reach that last balcony seat. Such booming tones, however, are overwhelming on video.

Not every actor who wants a tape made is celebrity material. When faced with such a situation, Albert says he does his best to make the performer look good. "If you notice that the profile is bad, you don't shoot from the side," he pointed out.

Don't be surprised that, even after giving your best work to a performer, he may be dissatisfied with the tape. In many cases, the performer is expressing displeasure with his own work, rather than with yours. "Most performers always feel that they can do better," said Albert Dabah, who said he experienced some of that same feeling when he was performing. It doesn't mean that the performer will avoid coming to you again. But you can help by coddling these clients a little bit, constantly encouraging them, and reassuring them that their videotape is a good one. When that videotape finally helps them to land the next job, they will believe you.

When videotaping a play, ballet, or other large-scale production, many videographers prefer to do the work during a dress rehearsal. It eliminates any problems that may occur when trying to shoot with an audience in attendance. In addition, if someone blows his line or forgets the words to the song, the action can be repeated.

It goes without saying that you should see the performance at least once before you do the videotaping. You don't want to be surprised by anything that happens.

Many of these shoots are done with one camera. Again, it depends on what the client is trying to achieve. Albert Dabah has done some videotaping of off-off-Broadway plays that were looking for investors to finance the production for an actual Broadway run. In those situations, Albert said the client does not expect the tape to resemble something you might see on TV. "The videotape is basically a selling tool," he said. For these jobs, Albert said, he uses one stationary camera that is able to take in the entire stage.

Other situations may call for two or three cameras, especially if you intend to intermingle wide shots with close-ups. It is a good idea to shoot with the director present, or with the person who has ordered the tape. He can then give you any special instructions as the play moves along.

Fashion shows present a certain challenge to the videographer. The runway shows staged by the top designers in New York are colorful and fast-moving. The models come strutting down the runway, often to disco music, swirling their skirts and flirting with the cameras. It is the video person's job to capture all the excitement of the show without losing sight of the tape's main purpose: to sell clothes.

It means that the cameraman must use several different camera angles. Some shots should take in the entire stage so the viewer can see the designer's entire presentation. Other shots should start at the model's head and finish at her feet to provide close inspection of the outfit. If the gown has a stand-out feature, a jeweled belt or plunging back, then the camera should zoom in on that.

Such fancy camera work must be done from one or more stationary cameras set up near the runway. Because the major fashion designers often show their new lines to packed houses, it is not possible for the videographer to move around once the show has started.

Covering fashion shows well is something that takes a great deal of experience. Many of the people who work in this area in New York, Paris, and Milan do nothing but videotape fashion shows. Chances are the shows that you plan to videotape will be on a smaller scale, possibly those held in your local department store. But you can benefit by the advice of one expert, Bill Marpett, who has worked in New York and Paris for Bill Blass, Calvin Klein, Ralph Lauren, and Albert Nipon.

As with any other video job, Bill first sits down with his client to determine what his expectations are. Often, what Bill can do depends on the client's budget. He can shoot with one camera or several. The most ambitious and most expensive project is to shoot several of the designer's shows with several cameras and then edit the best footage together.

Bill always looks at the clothing he will be shooting. If it's going to be a complicated shoot, then he takes his assistant director with him to make a list of the outstanding features on each garment. During the shoot, Bill will communicate with his cameramen through headphones and can instruct them which parts of each garment warrant close-ups. Bill considers this preproduction work crucial. "If there are a hundred and twenty pieces in a show, it's too much to think about," he said. "You have to be coordinated."

The major handicap to shooting fashion shows is the inability to move the camera. "It's like shooting in a strait-jacket," said Bill. "You have to do everything in zooms and tilts. Technically, it's very challenging for the cameraman. You have to bring out all the details with close-ups, but you have to be able to work fast enough and smooth enough to capture the whole thing."

Not only is the stage area crowded, but there is interference from still photographers using flashbulbs. According to Bill, there is no way to prevent these pops of light from showing up on tape. "In the beginning when you look at the tape, these flashes look awful," he said. "But when you look at it for a long time, you don't see the flashes."

Bill said that he rarely shoots people in the audience, even when a famous star or socialite is sitting up front. The reason is that often he will give the designer a raw, unedited tape. "You really can only take crowd shots when you have control and can edit it out later," he explained. "Why take the chance that someone is going to yawn?"

Another reason Bill avoids crowd shots is that many people leave these fashion shows before the end. The New York showings are scheduled close together, so someone may dash out of Bill Blass's show in order to get a good seat at Calvin Klein's. Whatever the reason, Bill does not want to show empty seats. In fact, he tries to make the end of the tape, when the designer comes out for his bows, as upbeat as possible. "We try to make every show look like a success," he said.

Of course the audience for your fashion show may be different. Especially when it is a small affair with an enthusiastic local audience, your client may want you to fit in some audience shots. He may want the faces of his loyal customers to be on that videotape when he replays it in his store.

Bill has some advice for anyone videotaping fashion. Co-operation from the designer, or the person who has commissioned the tape, is imperative. Remember, however, that right before a designer shows his new fall or spring line, he is apt to be overloaded with work and may be tense and irritable. The same might be true of the local store owner who has signed you on. It is not the best time to start making demands on his time, but if you want to get the best shoot possible, you must. "You have to find out from the designer what he wants to bring out," he said. If the designer has hired a choreographer, Bill will also review the show with him.

For Bill's purposes, the clothes are the stars. "You are really at the mercy of the clothing," he said. Your situation may be different, depending upon the person who has ordered the videotape. A local department store, for example, may also be interested in the videotape conveying the store's ambience to encourage more shoppers. You need to get specific instructions from your client.

Many videographers accustomed to shooting in studios have difficulty adjusting to the frenetic world of fashion shows. "They complain that it's not perfect, and they're right," said Bill. "But it's our job to adjust to that."

Once the entertainment bug has bitten some video entrepreneurs, they get the fever. They want to make it to the big time and see their video productions on TV.

Be aware before you start out that network TV is difficult for the videographer to break into. The major reason is that most programs on network television still are shot on film. It's possible to make the transition from video to film, but you will have to prove yourself all over again. Film is a different medium entirely, and since the competition there is probably even fiercer than in video, you could have a hard time.

However, increasingly, video is finding its way onto TV.

Network programs that rely on video include news, sports, and soap operas. Many commercials, especially local ones, are shot with video. And now the various cable channels are providing new opportunities for the videographer.

Once again, the competition in all these areas is rough. While it may be relatively easy to make commercials for local clients, landing a national advertiser will be more difficult. Most major corporations use New York advertising agencies. "The advertising agency will stay with the same production company for a long time," said Steve Sarabande. If you do produce a good number of local commercials your chances to break onto the national scene will be greater. You will have clients and videotapes to show what you can do.

For several years now, cable has been promising to open up grand new vistas for the video producer. But the results have been disappointing. A large portion of the United States still has not been wired for cable. Although the industry has produced some excellent cable channels, these services have had difficulty attracting paying subscribers or advertisers. Without those revenues, these channels do not have the funds they at first envisioned they would have to pay for original programming. Many cable channels, in fact, have closed or have reduced their hours of operation. "Everyone is setting their hopes on cable, but I haven't seen cable do any favors for the independent producer," said Carol Slatkin, co-owner of Spectra Video Services in Washington, D.C.

There are people producing programming for cable, but many of them have worked either in video production or in television for years. Bob McBride, who operates Earthrise Entertainment Inc. with his wife, Ann, had filmed documentaries as an independent producer and also worked for a TV station in Seattle. Bob now produces programming for CBN (the Christian Broadcasting Network). Bob said he will occasionally shoot film, but the bulk of his work these days is in video.

While Bob believes that cable channels are actively looking for product, he said that there also are a lot of suppliers. "It's still very competitive," he noted. Contacts, he believes, are a necessity. "The world turns around who you know," he said. "If you don't have good contacts, you're swimming in an unknown sea."

Your geographical location also is important. While nothing says you can't produce cable programming in the Midwest, Bob reports that it's difficult to remain in the mainstream if you're not in New York or Los Angeles.

Some entrepreneurs conclude after a time that while entertainment video can be exciting, challenging, and satisfying, it alone will never produce enough business to buoy up a video company. "You can't just stick to entertainment," said Steve Sarabande. "There's just not enough work."

You will have to decide whether entertainment is for you and whether you should devote yourself to it full time. Probably the best approach is to add entertainment gradually to the video jobs you already do. Once you find that you are devoting enough time to entertainment to make it profitable by itself, you can move to specialize.

9

Video in Law

Megamillionaire Ashforth Canterbury III wants to change his will. Ashforth, who made a fortune trading in pork bellies, is determined to cut off his no-good brother Axelrod. Ashforth's lawyer is concerned. His wealthy client has acquired a reputation for being eccentric. After Ashforth's death, his lawyer envisions Axelrod contesting the will, thus tying up Ashforth's estate for years. The solution? Ashforth's lawyer has his client videotaped reading his will, testifying himself that he is of sound mind and body, and explaining why he prefers to leave his fortune to the Bedford Village Geranium Association.

George Spectacle is an expert on aluminum widgets. He himself holds two patents for improvements to this device, and he has worked for three different companies who have manufactured widgets for sale to both the industrial and consumer markets. George feels very strongly about the shoddy workmanship evident in the Super Widget manufactured by the Kosmic Widget Co. He is not surprised by the number of people who have sued after being injured using one of these widgets. When he talks about the Kosmic Widget, George is articulate and impressive, surely the kind of expert witness that could influence a jury now that these suits are being brought to trial. The problem? Because of a heart condition, George is unable to fly from California to New York to appear at the trial. The solution? The plaintiff's lawyer arranges to have George's deposition videotaped in California so that the jury will get the full flavor of his testimony.

Two years ago, Justine Wright's automobile was rear-ended by a city bus. Justine is now paralyzed from the waist down. Her injury has completely altered her life, making even the most simple task difficult for her to perform. In her suit against the city, Justine's lawyers were searching for the proper way to illustrate Justine's situation to the jury. Her lawyers engaged a video company to videotape Justine through an average day, beginning with her getting out of bed in the morning, washing up, getting dressed, eating breakfast, and ending with her preparing for bed. The resulting tape was so compelling, the city opted to settle Justine's case out of court.

Jerome Rockaway was killed when his car was sitting on a railroad track and was hit by an oncoming train. Jerome's relatives filed suit alleging that the railroad company was at fault for not warning motorists by clearly marking the intersection. The train company officials contested the suit, saying that because of a sharp curve, trains were forced to travel at a slow speed before coming to the intersection, and that any motorist sitting in a car on the track would have sufficient warning, not only by seeing the oncoming train, but by hearing its whistle. To make its case in court, the train company reconstructed the events up until the accident by having a videographer sit in a car parked on the tracks and record what one would be able to hear and see from the car.

The legal profession is discovering the advantages of video. More lawyers are finding out that videotaped evidence can mean the difference between winning and losing. And in cases involving wills and accident victims, videotape can actually prevent a lengthy court battle. "There might be some trepidation because it's new, but nevertheless when we're surrounded by computers and word processors, one must enter that century along with everyone else," reflected Robert Kraut, an attorney and director of New York City's Department of Finance who is pioneering the use of videotape in his department. "One can maintain his black robes and still think as a modern person."

No one can accuse the legal profession of going Hollywood, however. Videotape is being used, but in a conservative manner. TV shows like "Perry Mason" and movies like *The Verdict* have created the misconception that everything happening in a courtroom or law office is dramatic and exciting. The manner in which these legal events are staged and filmed has helped to build that aura of suspense and intrigue:

The camera zooms in on the beautiful female defendant as she struggles to hold back the tears. There is a close-up shot of her hands nervously twisting a delicate lace handkerchief. The camera photographs her face from above, thus making her look even more vulnerable. The district attorney, as he conducts his fierce cross-examination, is photographed from a lower point looking upward to accentuate his powerful position.

All these techniques make for wonderful entertainment.

But for video people who regularly work videotaping for the legal profession, Hollywood's interpretation of the law bears little resemblance to the real world. Those working in this area agree that it is bursting with opportunity for video people. Yet most note that the primary function for videotape in the legal area is to inform, not entertain.

There are several different legal procedures that are now videotaped, the two most common being depositions and wills. In addition, video is being employed in unique new ways where a lawyer feels that seeing the evidence on videotape will make his case more compelling to the jury. One of these new art forms is called "day-in-the-life-of," and features an accident victim, like the fictitious Justine Wright, going about his or her normal daily routine to illustrate how the accident has changed his or her life. These tapes can be very convincing. Milton Lowenstein, president of Omnivideo in Arlington, Virginia, which specializes in legal work, claims that among the cases where he has done a day-in-the-life-of tape, 75 percent were settled out of court. He calls day-in-the-life-of tapes "a tremendously important tool for accident malpractice."

Many videographers also are busy reconstructing an accident or other event on tape for the jury or judge to view.

In all of these areas, the main purpose of the videotape is to inform, not entertain. That does not mean that these tapes should be boring or amateurish. It merely means that the videographer should avoid being overly dramatic. "It would be improper to do what '60 Minutes' does during an interview, focusing on someone's fingers drumming on the table," said Gregory Joseph, a partner in the New York City law firm of Fried, Frank, Harris, Shriver & Jacobson. "That would not be acceptable. That would be the video person injecting his perception and his personality into it."

Susan Dinter, the head of Philadelphia-based Vipro

Communications, has been videotaping depositions for about ten years, including many taken during lawsuits over agent orange, asbestos, and the swine flu vaccine. "There is a big difference between a producer producing a legal show for TV and someone producing a videotape deposition," she explained. "You can get some guy off the street, and if you can teach him what he can and cannot do, he's better than someone who wants to be creative. You cannot zoom in on the court reporter's hands or the stenotype machine though they do that on TV. It's like night and day."

Because most of these tapes are technically simple— focusing on a man seated behind a desk as he reads his will, for example—one does not need the technical skill of, say, someone who tapes fashion shows where models quickly strut down a runway swirling their dresses in the camera's eye. That is an advantage if you have little technical experience and want to get started in video.

Nevertheless, be advised that those who are successful in the field have worked hard to impress the legal profession because, as in most areas, a great deal of the work still comes through word-of-mouth. These videographers pride themselves on being fair ("What is good for one side should be good for the other side," said Susan Dinter), dependable, and consistent. And if taping depositions and wills becomes boring, they can satisfy their creative urges by taping reconstructions of accidents or taping accident victims in day-in-the-life-of films, an area that calls for extreme sensitivity and professionalism.

Many who are making it in this area specialize in legal video. A few are attorneys, although many attorneys themselves do not believe that a law degree is essential. "The lawyers are going to have the legal background necessary," said Gregory Joseph. "Obviously, you have to know what the local rules are."

If you are seriously considering a career in legal video, you first should educate yourself on the various legal procedures. For example, you should know that during a deposition a witness testifies under oath. The setting usually is a conference room, but many videographers have traveled to hospitals, doctors' offices, or private homes to videotape testimony. The usual procedure is for the witness to be questioned by a lawyer and then cross-examined by the attorney for the opposing side. A court reporter records the minutes either by shorthand or by using a stenographic machine.

What can be photographed during a deposition, and in what manner, is governed by state and federal rules. In some cases, the camera must be permanently fixed on the witness, so the jury does not see the attorneys but only hears their voices. But in states where the rules are more liberal, the attorneys may also be photographed and the videographer may be permitted to zoom in on various participants. Nonetheless, the camera work is extremely simplistic. "I would call video depositions a zero art form," said Jerry Friedland, manager of ASR Video Systems in New York. "There's no creativity required or intended. It's a factual way of delivering information to whoever might see it—a jury, a judge."

Not all lawyers are aware of what video could mean to their practice. If you want their business, it is up to you to demonstrate video's many advantages.

A video deposition is far more entertaining than the present manner in which the written deposition is presented to a jury, with two lawyers reading the transcript into the court record. "There's nothing that rivals the tedium induced by two lawyers reading questions and answers to the jury, other than washing one's hands in tepid water," said Gregory Joseph. "Juries don't like being read to. They much prefer having a show." Studies done by the legal profession have shown that juries pay more attention to a videotaped deposition than to one being read into the record. Added Attorney Joseph: "There is definitely a correlation between a juror's attentiveness and his retention."

Video depositions are more effective. "Normally if the accident victim is in the hospital, the lawyers would go in, take a deposition on paper, snap a few pictures, and those would be passed around to the jury," said Fred Russo, a video entrepreneur in Connecticut. "But to actually see and hear in the accident victim's own words what happened to him has much greater impact."

Milton Lowenstein, who once videotaped then President Jimmy Carter giving a deposition in the Robert Vesco case, agrees that the video deposition can help a lawyer's case. "The most important thing is credibility," he said. "When you're in court with a written transcript, how can you read the question the way the original guy read it? The whole thing is, do you believe this witness?"

And no court reporter taking dictation by hand or machine can touch the accuracy of a videotape. A videotaped record "is utterly incapable of refutation," said Gregory Joseph.

You can also point out to lawyers that video depositions can cut legal costs. "If you're in a tort case where there's been a propane gas explosion, with hundreds of people injured and many witnesses, with the court's discretion, it's possible to take forty or fifty depositions and edit it down to just portions, related to the salient facts from each deposition," said Gregory. "It's something that has been done."

"There's another advantage," he added. "In a propane explosion, where you are a defendant and you are going to need an expert to testify on the same basic facts in each case, you can get an order, and the court will designate representatives to depose your expert. You do direct examination, they do cross. You can use that tape in each of five hundred trials rather than having to schedule that witness each time."

Videographers complain most about the differing state rules that govern how they can shoot a deposition. Gregory Joseph recommends that you equip yourself with the Federal Judicial Center Guidelines. These may be obtained through the Federal Judicial Center in Washington, D.C. In addition, Gregory suggests you obtain a copy of local state rules. "In New York State, for example, the entrepreneur should know that he must have a digital clock that flashes seconds on the camera at all times," said Gregory. That time device is a precaution to prevent anyone editing something out of the videotape.

But, as Jerry Friedland discovered, New York's digital clock rule does not apply in all states. "We did a deposition recently for an attorney in North Carolina," Jerry recalled. "We told him what New York State required, including the date and time generator. He told us the case would not be tried in New York and that he did not want the date and time generator. Also he said he wanted the lens to move in and out occasionally to break up the monotony of staring at one person on the screen." As a result of that experience, Jerry said he relies for the most part on the attorneys to tell him what they want.

How much should you depend on the lawyer who has hired you? "There's an awful lot of ignorance among lawyers in this field," admitted Gregory Joseph, who has used video in some of his cases and written articles for legal publications on the subject. While you may be reluctant to interpret the law for a lawyer who is paying your fee, at the same time you want to make sure the videotape you produce will be admissible in court. You can't build up a reputation if no one ever sees your work.

Gregory believes the best way to correct a lawyer would be to come equipped with a copy of the state rules and the federal judicial guidelines. "Once that's clear, there shouldn't be a problem," said Gregory.

Remember, you are the video expert, and shouldn't be reluctant to tell the lawyer how you think the deposition should be taped. Milton Lowenstein, who has been taping depositions since 1974, is one who has definite ideas. "We set up a conference table," he said. "The calling attorney sits on the left of the witness. The defending attorney for that deposition sits on the right. The cameraman is on the other end facing the witness." Lowenstein always takes an assistant with him.

Lowenstein's cardinal rule: "Never lose the witness. He is on camera one hundred percent of the time. The only exception is if the witness is demonstrating an X ray or chart and he has a pointer and you want to get in close to what he's doing."

But that does not mean that the witness should be the only person on camera. "If that particular jurisdiction will allow you to show an opening shot, then you do," said Milton. "You show the two attorneys while the director is cueing the witness. After the director is finished, you show the cross-examining position." Working within the confines of the state rules, Milton Lowenstein noted, "You have to use a little judgment about how to get away from the doldrums."

He points out that lawyers and judges still are pretty conservative in what they want from a videotape. "Judges I have spoken to have told me very simply, 'We want only one camera. No Hollywood business about getting dramatic results and if the witness has a blemish or a physical drawback, don't zoom in and show that.' If it's part of what you would see from the jury box, fine, but nothing to accentuate anyone's deficiencies."

The Arlington-based videographer is, nonetheless, critical of this conservatism. "Some jurisdictions like Michigan and Illinois want the witnesses shot only from the navel up," he said. "It sounds good to the lawyer until he has a case and discovers that half the jurors are asleep."

Susan Dinter agrees that it sometimes is difficult to stay within the guidelines and still produce an interesting videotape. "You don't want to bore the jury," she said. "If you have the camera on the witness at all times, the jury will lose its attention span and get bored and will resent having to sit there and stare at a picture in a box. People are not used to that. They're used to commercial TV."

Yet Susan said she works hard to make the videotape fair to both sides. That means holding off on close-ups and zooms. "If a doctor is showing an X ray you can use an extreme close-up," she said. "But if he has a whole series of X rays on the shadow box and he's referring to the first one, unless he points to it, it should never be the camera operator who makes the decision that he is definitely referring to number one."

Susan is one who believes that specializing in the legal area has helped her hone her skill. "You need a good understanding of what a deposition is," she explained. "It's not just knowing that a witness comes into a room and two attorneys can ask him questions like he's on a witness stand. That's not enough." Certain standard questions can be lengthy. When the lawyer poses such a question, Susan often pulls back to capture both the attorney and the witness. After the lawyer completes the question, she might do a slow zoom in on the witness.

Most videographers are careful about how they use the zoom while taping a deposition. "It's never a fast zoom, like the ones in soap operas on TV if the star starts to cry," said Susan. She noted that, in video depositions, rarely would there be an extreme close-up.

Because legal videographers are dealing with sensitive material when they tape depositions, many say they have taken out insurance to protect themselves. To be cautious, you should do the same. After all, you are dealing with lawyers, and what profession would be more apt to sue you over a botched job? "Since it's a brand new field, and since you're going to be videotaping people who are dying and the trial maybe won't come up for two to four years, you must have malpractice insurance," said Susan. She has malpractice insurance for occurrence of unusual errors and omissions. She also has included all her employees and subcontractors under the protection. Susan admits the cost is high, but believes that because there is no precedent in this field, the price is worth it.

Susan also noted that she makes several copies of the videotape for the attorneys to use. Nonetheless, she never lets the original tape out of her possession without requiring the party who is taking the tape to sign a release.

Videotaping wills is less complicated than videotaping depositions. The concept still is a new one, and video wills are not acceptable in all states. Even some videographers feel the whole concept is ghoulish. "Personally I wouldn't want a video will," said Bill Hood, head of Custom Video Productions in Clearwater, Florida. "I wouldn't want to see one of my sisters or my mother on videotape after she had passed away."

Yet many videographers and legal experts believe the video will could become commonplace. "The very nature of the word 'will' is to try to preserve the individual's own will and how he would have liked his own estate to be distributed," said Robert Kraut. At present, witnesses are called upon to witness the signing of the will. "The sole purpose of witnesses, if they are called, is to raise their right hands and say the person was in his right mind when he wrote this will," explained Robert. "Rather than ask strangers, what better presentation to determine someone's will than to see a videotape of him talking, answering certain questions, demonstrating his own will. Saying, 'Yes, if I were alive I would want so-and-so to get $100,000, and I want that son-of-a-gun of a brother of mine not to get a dime because he did terrible things to my mother.' If that's your purpose—to have someone speak from the grave—what better than a visual presentation?"

According to Richard Love, a video entrepreneur in Maryland, lawyers who contact his company want to videotape wills for various reasons. "In one instance, they were making modifications to a will," he recalled. "They felt there were questions that might arise at a later date if the will was probated as to what frame of mind this person was in when he made the modifications, whether he was sound of mind and body. That can be documented with videotape."

Most videographers use only one stationary camera to tape a video will. Usually, the person is seated behind a table. "What happens on the tape is that the person reads the will and comments about why he or she is making these changes," said Richard, who says that he takes an assistant with him to do the taping. Others present would include the lawyer and the two witnesses. The person signs the will on camera, as do the two witnesses.

Because a will by its nature is a very personal document, some videographers offer to leave the room after they have the camera set up and running. Some videographers leave of their own accord when the proceedings become too acrimonious. "You wouldn't believe some of these people," said Bill Hood, who has taped many wills in Florida. "They actually get back at people on videotape."

Without a video will, if an ousted heir challenges the will, the deceased person's lawyer would resort to obtaining affidavits from the witnesses, attesting to the dead person's sound state of mind at the time he drew up his will. But as

Robert Kraut pointed out, the lawyer sometimes has a hard job finding those witnesses. Often, they themselves have passed away. Under the new method, "the judge and the attorney can sit in chambers and watch the video will and determine, was there undue influence here, was he merely eccentric or was he insane," said Robert.

In recent years there has been much publicity surrounding the wills of famous people like Groucho Marx, Darryl F. Zanuck, and others, whose heirs contested the distribution of the wealth. Robert Kraut believes that video wills could eliminate this litigation. "The burden would now shift to the other party who says this person who died was insane," he said. "If one is going to make that allegation, one had better support it because of the visual evidence left by the deceased."

Kraut would take this whole area one step further. Because so many of these fights over inheritances center on a new spouse fighting with the deceased's children over the estate, why not have a videotape made at the time of the wedding? Then the wealthy spouse can declare his or her intentions, either to leave the estate to the new spouse or to leave it to the children.

Day-in-the-life-of tapes are viewed as another way of avoiding a lengthy court trial. In most instances, the plaintiff is an accident victim. The purpose of these tapes is to illustrate for the judge and jury what the injury means to the plaintiff in terms of carrying on his daily routine.

"Day-in-the-life films are generally accepted now, although ten years ago, that was not the case," pointed out Gregory Joseph. Still, you should follow certain guidelines to ensure that the videotape will be allowed in court.

Generally, you will be engaged by the plaintiff's attorney. At this point, you should receive from the lawyer all the pertinent facts that you will need to plan the shoot. Is the victim ambulatory? Is the injured party's home dark? Will extra lighting be needed? Make it a point to visit the accident victim's home several days before the shoot to acquaint yourself with the layout.

Some videographers say they are reluctant to plan the tape too much for fear that it could be ruled inadmissible because it was scripted. One videographer even claimed that he advises the attorney in the case not to be present so that if the videographer is called upon later to testify as to the circumstances surrounding the making of the tape, he can say that he and the plaintiff were not coached.

However, attorney Gregory Joseph scoffed at that notion. He maintained that a videographer should not be reluctant to depend heavily on the lawyer for direction. "A lawyer should be present," he stated. "Anything the video person does will directly affect the relevance of that tape and the video person is generally unqualified to determine what he should or shouldn't be doing. It's really important that the lawyer be there. The absence of the lawyer is not going to enhance admissibility one iota."

In addition, Gregory said that the videographer is definitely permitted to tell the accident victim what he wants to see and the details should be worked out with the lawyer in advance. "If they want to see a normal routine, he can ask whether that involves getting up in the morning, brushing teeth, putting on clothes, cooking meals," he said. "You definitely have to coordinate it. There has to be a director there, and if not the lawyer, then the video expert. It should look to be professionally done as a documentary. It shouldn't appear that things are being done in a random manner. Whether in chronological order or if it's done by way of demonstrating how one copes with certain activities, it should appear to have some theme to it."

Experts advise not to ask the accident victim to engage in

strenuous activities that will make him grimace or appear to be in extreme pain. Oftentimes, videotapes that are heavy-handed will be disallowed. "The lower key and the better taste, the more effective it will be," said Gregory Joseph.

Gregory also recommends that you be sure of what you want to shoot the first time. "Don't do a lot of outtakes and have the victims redo the scenes," he advised. "That tape will be subject to discovery by the other side and may lead to questions as to the purposes and intent demonstrated by the outtakes. Things shouldn't be done haphazardly, because anything that's said is something that can go into court as well."

Gregory admitted that when a videographer is doing a day-in-the-life-of tape, the aesthetics have to be subordinated since the main purpose is to inform, not entertain. However, he emphasized that the tape should keep the interest of the jury. "It should be done in a professional-looking manner," he said. "If the tape looks to be done with a hand-held camera that's very jerky, it's going to be displeasing and it's going to distract from the contents." That could mean using a tripod to avoid a shaky camera.

Omnivideo is one company that treats day-in-the-life-of tapes with the professionalism they deserve. Milton Lowenstein said he has one cameraman who excels in this area. "This cameraman is very soft-spoken and sensitive," said Milton. "Kids love him. He also knows how to hold a camera." In addition, Milton said he himself is present at all times in the event he must testify in court.

While courts are increasingly liberal in accepting day-in-the-life-of tapes, it is more difficult to gain admission for tapes that attempt to reconstruct the circumstances surrounding an accident. The reason, according to Gregory Joseph, is that unless the exact situation that existed at the time of the accident can be duplicated, the opposing side has a good opportunity for getting the videotape thrown out of court.

Nevertheless, some videographers are keeping busy doing such tapes. Susan Dinter, for example, has helped to reconstruct the scenes of several accidents. In product liability cases, for example, Susan may go to the work site and videotape the machinery. "Some piece of equipment may be too large to be brought into court," she said. "We'll shoot on location."

Whether one wants to videotape depositions, wills, day-in-the-life-of tapes, or accident reconstructions, how do you get started in this specialized area? First of all, while many people are restricting themselves to video legal services, whether you can afford to do so depends upon where you live. In New York and Washington, for example, where there is a lot of legal work, such a specialty might make sense. But in a smaller city or town, it may prove to be a quick road to bankruptcy.

The best method may be to add videotaping depositions and wills to what you already do. That way, you can build a reputation in the legal area without cutting off your other clients. If there proves to be enough legal business and you find it is the area that really captures your fascination, then you can narrow your business.

Most videographers say that the best way to get started is by associating yourself with a court reporting service. Most lawyers still insist that a written record be kept in addition to the video record. "Even though the federal rules of civil procedure permit depositions to be videotaped without a stenographic record, it is extremely rare that a lawyer wants it that way," said Gregory Joseph. "The stenographic record is extremely convenient for all sorts of trial preparation purposes, particularly, but not exclusively, when you have a videotape."

"One thing you do when you're planning a cross-examination, you go through the deposition and plot out those questions critical to your case which the other side has answered correctly," Gregory said. "You know you will ask him those at trial. If he answers the questions differently, you have to be able to go immediately to that print. Not having a transcript makes it tedious to locate it on the tape."

Many court reporting services put great stock in the idea that the legal profession will always need a written record and have resisted the idea of adding video to their services. That fact works to your advantage because when a client requests a videotape, the court reporting service must find a qualified expert, and that expert could be you.

Jerry Friedland of ASR Video Systems reports that his company receives some of its business through court reporting services. And he returns the favor to ensure that those jobs keep coming. "If we get a cold inquiry that also requires a stenographer, we would call one that we have worked with over the years," he said.

Jerry also reports that some of his video legal business comes from clients that he has served in other ways. "If one of these clients calls and says he needs a video deposition made, we find out exactly what he needs," he said.

You might try to educate local lawyers on video in law by asking to address a meeting of the local bar association. Or you might get a listing of the local lawyers through the local bar association or even in the Yellow Pages, and do a mailing. Remember that most members of the legal profession are still unaware of video's advantages. You must convince them.

One fact most people involved in legal video agree upon: It is an area that will continue to grow. "The growth of video will be slow and steady," said Jerry Friedland, who feels confident that "there is an awareness factor and an education factor that will continue the growth."

10

Video in Business

FOR MANY corporations, using video is a business decision that makes sense. Video can help a company reduce its costs, increase its customers, enhance its public image, and improve employee morale. Communications experts expect more corporations to embrace video in the years ahead once they are made fully aware of this medium's potential.

Already, corporate work is keeping more than one video entrepreneur in operation. Some videographers prefer corporate work to consumer work for several reasons. Corporations, more than consumers, mean repeat business. The compensation can be greater, especially if the job involves covering a lengthy convention. And, many videographers find corporate executives easier to work with than consumers.

Still, many video people manage to keep a mix of corporate and consumer work. Corporate work often leads to consumer work, and vice versa. If you are shooting a wedding, for example, the father of the bride may be the chief executive at a major corporation who will be so impressed with your talents he will want to engage you for a job with his company. Likewise, a corporate president who is pleased with your work may decide to have you videotape one of his private parties. This reciprocity is one reason you should keep an open mind and never forget promotion when you are out in public.

Many videographers, in fact, stumbled onto the corporate scene without planning. After several jobs, however, they discovered they enjoyed corporate work and decided to actively promote themselves in it.

Business video does not have the glamour of entertainment video and it may lack the human interest element present in consumer video or video dating. But corporate video does provide other rewards. Besides the financial compensation and possible repeat business, video people report becoming so involved in the subject matter of some business projects that they have actually pursued the topics on their own later on.

If a corporate video job does not come falling into your lap, then you will have to go after this business on your own. Should you approach large or small companies? Either one could make use of video. In the beginning, it's probably best to make a list of area companies, regardless of size, that you would like to work for.

Once you have this list, you can put together a mailing to tell these companies about your service. Take a little extra time to locate the right person within each company who would be able to act on your information. Otherwise, your hard work is likely to end up in the wastebasket.

How do you locate this person? Be aware that many major corporations now have their own video units. Some of these video departments are huge and completely fulfill the corporation's video needs. But in some cases these departments employ a small staff that they supplement by hiring outside videographers for individual jobs. You want to locate the person who heads this department. He may be the key that will unlock many video opportunities for you.

Perhaps the large company you are writing to does not have a video unit. It probably will have a public relations office. The person who heads up this office is usually in charge of publicity and other activities involving the media. The public relations office will retain an outside videographer whenever the need arises. Also, anyone within the company who wants to use video would call the public relations office for suggestions. Once this person knows about your service, not only will he be able to use you, but also he may recommend your service to others.

It would be a good idea to write to both the video department and the public relations department, provided a corporation has both. Often, these units operate independently of each other, and both could prove to be sources of video jobs.

Many corporations employ outside public relations firms to handle their affairs for them. You can find these firms listed in the Yellow Pages, and it would be wise to include them in your mailing. These firms are constantly looking for video production people they can use or recommend to others.

If a company does not have a public relations office and you would still like to include them, then your best bet is to write to the person responsible for marketing and sales. This executive most likely organizes sales meetings to educate employees and also arranges presentations to customers. He may never have thought about using video, but may be easy to convince on the advantages. For a small company, possibly one that is family-run, you should direct your mailing to the top executive.

When compiling your mailing list, take the extra time to make phone calls and check that you have the right names. Nothing turns off a businessperson more than receiving a letter in which his name or title is incorrect.

Your mailing should look professional and be clear and

concise. Try to keep your message to one page. You should outline your services, detail any recent important corporate work you have done, and include any references from other companies you may have worked for (after clearing the recommendation with them, of course). Make sure to include your name and phone number. After a reasonable amount of time has elapsed, you should follow up with a phone call.

Your objective is to get an appointment with an executive in charge of hiring videographers. Once you are in the door, you want to impress this person with your video abilities. How do you do that? Listen to the criteria used by one such executive, Steve Lokker, manager of employee communications for Pratt & Whitney, an aircraft manufacturer that is a division of United Technologies Corp. Steve hires dozens of videographers each year and will spend anywhere from thirty minutes to two hours with a video person listening to his sales pitch. "I don't listen to them out of courtesy," said Steve. "My time is too valuable to waste by entertaining people and raising their expectations."

Steve says he looks for professionalism in the video person's approach, and sometimes the small details count. Steve questioned the seriousness of one organization that came in without any printed literature about the company, not even business cards. (Printed material always is a good idea since the business executive can review it later on. It will help him remember you and your company.)

On another occasion, Steve recalled, two women came in to discuss their new video company. One woman did all the talking and never introduced her associate. Later, when Steve received material on the company, it turned out the silent partner was in fact the owner. Needless to say, Steve was puzzled about who was actually in charge and chose not to deal with them.

Keep in mind that when dealing with business people

you should observe the courtesies and practices that they expect of others they do business with.

Appearance is important. You may go trudging around your studio in a torn shirt and jeans, but don't show up for an appointment with a business executive in such an outfit. When the executive comes out to meet you, a good, firm handshake is in order. You should introduce anyone you have brought along, and explain his association with your company.

Time is of the essence. Come prepared. Steve was most impressed with one man who came in with a briefcase containing a video recorder and videotape that explained everything about the company quickly and efficiently. "He came equipped with everything he needed to sell me," said Steve.

Steve said he looks for videographers who are concerned with the contents of the videotape. "Anybody can run a camera, edit a videotape, and put in music," said Steve. "But I'm not going to spend my money on razzle-dazzle. The message and the context are what interest me." Steve says he is not particularly impressed with video people who have experience in network television or commercials, but he does look for people who have done a variety of things.

Those who are well equipped have an edge with Steve. "If they do their own editing, it means they don't have to rent from other people whom I will end up paying for," Steve said. If you don't have your own postproduction facilities, you may want to assure the business executive that this will not be a problem. Perhaps you can point out that you have access to low-cost editing facilities, provided that is the case.

After you have met with a corporate executive like Steve, be sure to follow up. These officials are busy and some things tend to fall between the slats. Don't let your video company be one of them. Be persistent.

What types of video services can you offer business? Actually, these jobs can run the gamut and may be similar to jobs you do for consumers, entertainers, or lawyers.

Each year a corporation may have several social gatherings that they would like to have videotaped. These tapes can be used when putting together a presentation about the company for sales or recruiting, or to show employees at the next social event.

These social affairs are similar to consumer parties with one important difference. Since the videotape is being made for a distinct purpose (the consumer tapes are merely to entertain), you should get specific marching orders from the person who commissioned the tape. What is he trying to accomplish with the videotape? Are there certain activities (a toast, a receiving line, the arrival of an important guest) that you must be sure not to miss? Are there certain people who should be photographed more than others?

You will not want to operate on a hit-or-miss basis. Every corporation has its own pecking order, and you want to make sure to include as many shots as possible of those at the top. It would be a good idea to meet as many of these people ahead of time as you can. You also may want to come equipped with still photographs of the executives so that you will not miss them in the crowd.

Find out whether there will be decorations that prominently feature the name of the corporation. You might want to take shots of banners, favors, or anything else that has the name of the company printed on it. Later, you can edit these shots into the tape, thus reminding the viewer of the company name.

Every year, companies and associations hold thousands of conventions around the country. Haven McKinney, a videographer who works in Washington, D.C., keeps in touch with the city's convention center so that he knows which groups are meeting when. It's a good idea to contact these groups far enough in advance so that they can have time to consider any proposal you might make.

These conventions have as their central purpose the dissemination of large quantities of information. A major convention can feature hundreds of speakers delivering technical speeches. Most conventions also allow time for relaxation and entertainment.

Increasingly the videographer is being called upon to capture the spirit and substance of these meetings. How you cover a convention will vary depending upon what the company or association wants to do with the tape. Again, it is important to get specific instructions so that you will not end up missing something your client considers crucial to the success of the tape.

Often the videotape will be used primarily as an educational tool for those who could not attend the convention. In such cases, you will be expected to focus on the important speakers. Remember that an informative tape can still be interesting and entertaining. You don't want to put your audience to sleep (even if several of the speakers did). You can use your video expertise to liven things up, possibly adding music if your client approves.

If the tape will be used for promotion, then you should make the conference look even more exciting. Good editing can help to pick up the pace. As long as your client does not care about imposing a minimum length for each person's speech, you can select the cogent comments, and omit the rest.

Always try to obtain the printed text of a speaker's remarks as far in advance as possible. You can then review his speech and note areas where he may be using slides, charts, or other visual aids. Find out whether the speaker plans to lower the lights in the room. You will have to compensate for that when shooting.

When videotaping the speakers, make sure to capture

enough audience reaction shots, also known as cutaways. Later these close-ups can be edited in, especially when you are showing a speaker whose audience fell asleep. You can edit in more alert-looking individuals. "Cutaways can bail you out," said John Fama, president of Famavision and Fama II Productions. One cautionary note, however. Be certain when you add these cutaways that the individual's response is in sync with what the speaker is saying. You don't want to show someone laughing if the lecturer is detailing the mortality rates for various cancers.

Covering a convention can be exhausting. You are running from event to event just like a delegate. Chances are you will toil around the clock, since most conventions hold meetings during the day and banquets at night. You will be trying to get as much on videotape as possible, because editing alone will not put in shots you don't have. In the words of one official, "You have to have good eggs to make a good omelet."

Try not to lose your sense of humor. There's even a way of showing your sense of humor through videotape. One videographer reportedly put together a separate videotape that included all the muffed lines, censored remarks, and otherwise embarrassing moments that occurred during the convention. It not only amused his clients, but it illustrated for them what a skillful editing job he had done, since the final tape showed each person at his best.

When a corporation has a major announcement, it naturally would like the event covered by the local television stations. In many instances, however, the station manager is reluctant to tie up a camera crew for half a day just to use a few minutes of videotape from a company. The situation is different if the company provides the station with a videotape of the press conference, meeting, or whatever. Then the station can use the tape without incurring any expenses.

At the same time the company is pleased because it has received the publicity.

These videotapes, which have become known as video press releases, are distributed to both broadcast and cable TV channels. Such tapes can be in several different forms: video with no sound, video with voice-over, and the complete video and audio just as the event occurred.

Steve Lokker said Pratt & Whitney often employs the video press release and hires outside videographers to do them. "We reach an audience of six to ten million every time we do a video press release," he said. Steve said he meets with the video people beforehand, explains the project to them, and gives them as much information as he has. Sometimes Steve's office will prepare the script; other times the video people do the scripting with Steve's office handling any revisions.

Emhart Corporation, a diversified manufacturing company based in Connecticut, produced a video version of its annual report. Other corporations have expressed interest in this idea, and it may be something you will want to sell to your clients. You would illustrate through videotape some of the highlights of a company's business year. The videocassette could then be distributed to the press, stockholders, and employees.

Corporations and even unions are beginning to investigate video as a means for communicating with their employees and members. Carol Slatkin, co-owner of Spectra Video Services in Washington, D.C., produces an internal video newsletter for the AFL-CIO called the "Labor Video Bulletin." It comes out twice a month and attempts to keep union members apprised of activities around the country.

Video can also be used to train employees better. With the technological revolution taking over the country, employees are being asked to operate electronic office equipment and other gadgets. Ultimately, they are told, these devices will make their jobs easier. But the initial reaction is one of fear and mistrust.

Corporations that manufacture this new equipment are discovering that it often takes more than a user's manual to give an employee enough information to operate a complicated piece of machinery properly. It is too expensive to send a sales representative out to give instructions after every sale. It is more cost-effective to make a videotape that will give the customer all the information he needs to operate and maintain the equipment. "Industry has found that video is very useful for training," said Skip Winitsky, of Media/Arts Management Associates in Washington, D.C. "You can get the same information to all the people in the hierarchy."

The videotape is practical because eventually the salesman has to pack up and go home. The videotape can be kept and referred to for a refresher course, or in the event a new employee who is unfamiliar with the office product comes on board.

These instructional tapes are not restricted to office machinery. They are also used in heavy industry to show workers how to use new equipment properly. In many of these cases, the focus is on safety. Companies believe that these videotapes can help to prevent on-the-job accidents. Rather than being handed a complicated manual, the worker can actually see someone using the new machine.

In the event that a worker is injured when using the equipment and sues the company for negligence, the training videotape can be used to show a judge or jury that the company took adequate precautions in warning its employees of possible hazards. Many videographers who specialize in legal work also do training tapes simply because of the likelihood that these tapes will be used in court.

Of course, training tapes do not have to include any

equipment or machinery. In fact, as the United States moves away from heavy industries toward service industries, more of these training videotapes will show employees how to provide a service. Skip Winitsky has done several of these service videotapes. One for a banking association showed its members how to lobby Congress effectively for passage of legislation. Another that Skip did for employees of an accounting firm illustrated how to handle an Internal Revenue Service audit for a client. Such a videotape would be used by the accounting firm to instruct its accountants all over the country. "These videotapes are very effective," said Skip.

With most training videotapes, whether they involve a demonstration of machinery or play-acting by the participants, it is important to work with a script. "If they haven't scripted it out, we plan it ourselves," said John Fama. In one case, John brought in a creative consultant who devised the approach John was looking for. Without a script, you will waste time, videotape, and money, and the final product may not meet anyone's expectations.

You should understand what the client intends to do with the videotape. If machinery is involved, you should understand how it works and what features you should be focusing on. John Fama emphasizes that you should not lose any of the audio, because anything said during a demonstration could be important.

John also advises that you get extra close-up shots that you can edit in later just in case they're needed. Once John has turned his camera on during the videotaping of a demonstration, he just lets it roll. Anything he captures may be valuable. And, if not, "you can edit it out in the end."

Competition for jobs these days is fierce and every candidate is looking for that extra edge that will put his name at the top of the list. Some of these job applicants are firmly convinced that a video résumé will do just that.

There is no doubt that seeing someone talk about himself and his qualifications on videotape can be more impressive if the person makes an effective presentation. From the viewpoint of the person who is doing the hiring, it can also cut down on the time spent interviewing dozens of people. In-person interviews are bound to take up a certain amount of an executive's time. There are the introductory pleasantries, the obligatory questions, and the inevitable office tour. But that same executive could watch two minutes of a videotape, decide against the applicant, yank the videocassette out of the videotape player, and have used only a few minutes of his time.

From the applicant's point of view, a videotaped presentation may give him the opportunity to demonstrate talents or talk about subjects he may never be asked about in an interview. Perhaps the applicant is a fabric designer. On videotape he could show some of his creations in living color. If he is seeking a position as a creative person in an advertising agency, his visual and audio compositions could be presented. The applicant could be taped in his own office or in an environment where he feels comfortable, thus adding to the appeal of the interview. And, since videotaped résumés are still such a novelty, what executive could resist watching one?

Video résumés are a novelty now, but many experts believe the concept could become commonplace in the near future. The advantages are obvious. Currently corporations pay to fly in job applicants from all over the country. While many of these people are eventually hired, many more are ruled out after a few minutes of that initial interview. A company could save time and money by cutting these people before it has paid for their plane fares. The applicants, meanwhile, would not waste their time flying to interview with companies that will not invite them back.

Where do you find the people interested in video résumés? There are several places to look. Recent graduates of colleges and graduate schools will soon be job hunting. You should visit some of your local colleges and talk to someone in charge of placement. Let them know about your service so that they may inform students. You should also think about advertising in college publications and professional journals.

One videographer in Washington, D.C., said he has been approached by an employment agency that specializes in placing high level executives. This video expert will be doing video résumés for the agency. There are probably employment agencies in your own city that could offer video with their services. A well-written letter outlining your service could convince them.

Think about making a demonstration videotape that you can show interested people. If you have yet to videotape your first résumé, then shoot a demonstration using a volunteer. You may even want to show several short résumés to give the viewer an idea of what can be done on videotape.

There are several ways you can approach the video résumé. How you do will depend on the qualifications and camera presence of the individual. Someone who is confident and self-assured and photographs well may be best presented talking to the camera about his qualifications and job experience. Another person may do better in a question and answer format with you or an assistant posing the queries that have been carefully scripted ahead of time.

It is best to keep the final videotape as short as possible. Keep in mind that one advantage of the video résumé is that it can save time. You don't want to nullify that by presenting a videotape that is thirty minutes long. The length should depend on the applicant and what he has to say. Here is another area where a script will help.

Videotape allows the job applicant to actually see how he

looks to others. It is a great way to practice for that important job interview. In addition to résumés, many videographers are using video to help people improve their performance. A person can see right off what he is doing wrong—slouching, stammering, nodding his head too much—without being told. But as the video expert, there are other things you may be able to advise.

Eye contact with the interviewer is important. Also, the subject shouldn't be overly aggressive. Even if he is the former chairman of a major corporation, he is now seeking another job and should avoid appearing as if he is still holding the reins. Such behavior is bound to turn off the interviewer. Seeing himself on videotape also allows the job seeker to practice replies to standard questions. A major stumbling block to many is a truthful answer to the age-old question, "Why did you leave your last job?" Rehearsing his response will give both you and your client the opportunity to judge whether his answer is credible.

"We have convinced a good many real estate agents that video is the way to go," said Bill Hood of Custom Video Productions, who says the key is to persuade the agent of video's value as a sales tool. "Real estate is dog-eat-dog," he said. "You have to have something better than your competition. If you're offering video, that's something the competition down the street might not be offering."

Video in real estate is especially useful when the agent is trying to sell a home to a client living in another city or state. If that client has access to a videocassette recorder (and most people these days do), then the agent can send him the tapes of those homes that meet his requirements. He can then narrow down his selection, because chances are when he arrives in town to view homes he will be operating on a tight time schedule and will not wish to waste time seeing homes unsuitable for him and his family.

Videotaping for real estate agents is an ongoing business, which is one reason it is an attractive one for you. If video works for the agent, he will be selling more homes and getting more clients, and more homes for you to videotape.

The key is to get your foot in the door. You may try a direct mail campaign or try phoning some local agents to tell them about your service. Be warned ahead of time that many real estate agents put great stock in their selling ability. Make it clear to these agents that video does not replace such sales talent, it merely makes better use of it. Purely and simply, video can save time, and in real estate, as in most businesses, time is money.

One videographer described hospitals as "virgin territory" for video. There are many applications for video in medicine—training tapes for the hospital staff, security tapes for hospital personnel, educational and demonstration tapes for patients, and entertainment tapes that can be shown over a closed circuit TV system for viewing in patients' rooms.

Yet there are reasons video is not enjoying widespread use in hospitals. The primary reason is financial. Most hospitals just do not have the money to spend on video, even though such an investment could save money in the long run while at the same time improving the quality of health care for many people. When there is money available, the medical staff will assign video a low priority. Medical equipment and other items come first. "The medical market is young, but there is a lot of intimidation about breaking into it," said Bernie Block, who is head of video production for a New York City medical center.

Bernie basically runs a one-person department with a small budget, yet he has managed to do some innovative things in medical video. In his spare time, Bernie also has formed his own company, Block Burns Inc., to specialize in medical video. "If you're an innovative person and you're not interested in big profits, go into health care," Bernie advised.

There is a way to get around the lack of hospital funds. Some videographers are approaching major corporations who supply products to hospitals. Many of these companies can be convinced to fund a videotape that would be viewed by hospital patients. The videotape would prominently feature the company's products.

For example, a videotape on baby care would show the new mother using disposable diapers, baby lotion, baby powder, diaper rash ointment, and other items all manufactured by one company.

Most hospitals hold classes for new mothers on baby care, and a videotape could either supplement those instructions or replace them. A mother could view the tape at her own convenience rather than having to rush to make a certain class. A videotape also could save the time of hospital personnel who could then be used more effectively to deal with more serious patient problems.

As a starter, you may want to approach the director of your local hospital to find out his attitude toward video. Perhaps he may be intrigued enough to find the funds for a small project.

If you have no luck with hospitals, look at corporations. When you do a mailing, set aside those companies that manufacture products used in hospitals—drug and pharmaceutical companies are obvious choices—for a special pitch about using videotapes in hospitals.

Dealing with corporations will be different from dealing with consumers or entertainers. It is important, therefore, that you develop the proper attitude when dealing with business people.

Remember, you are interested in repeat business. Losing

a corporation as a client is not like losing a consumer (although a good videographer would not want to lose either one). A corporation consists of many people and if the word spreads that your work was substandard, it could hurt your relationship with other companies. Also, if a company rejects your work, you stand to lose a substantial amount of business.

Especially when you are starting out, it might be worth going that extra mile just to be sure that an important company returns. "I won't let anyone go away unhappy," said John Fama. "I sat here for three days with one man who ended up sleeping in my office. But when he left he was satisfied with the job we did."

To conclude with a summary and recap: Preproduction planning is very important with corporate clients. Many will have scripted out the job, but if they haven't, you should do it for them. You should obtain the complete schedule of the event you are to videotape. Say it's a seminar. Go down the list of speakers with the client. Which ones does he consider crucial? Which ones not so important?

This means sitting down with the client and interviewing him about what he hopes to accomplish with the videotape. Who are the key players in his little drama? Will the tape be for in-house use, or will it get widespread exposure outside the company? Does he expect music and special effects?

Some corporations are easier to deal with than others. In some companies, every decision has to be approved by several different executives. This decision-making process can hold you up. When you agree to take the job, make sure you know who and how many people you will be answering to. If necessary, you may have to get a time limit written into your contract just to speed things up.

In fact, it's a good idea to spell out all your obligations in the contract, just in case personnel changes at the corporation put your project in jeopardy. You want to make sure that it's the corporation, not some individual, that has approved the project.

Learn to cultivate corporate executives. After you have finished a videotape, call the official you worked with. Find out what other things he is working on. Perhaps you can suggest a use for video that could enhance one of his new ventures. Encourage him to mention your service to others.

When the time comes for you to decide whether to specialize, corporate video is one area that you could easily choose. Even if you decide to continue handling a variety of video jobs, a good supply of lucrative corporate assignments can help give your company the support it needs.

11

Video as Matchmaker

THERE ARE now more than 50 million single adults in the United States and the government predicts that by 1990 half of all United States households will be headed by a single person. This has not escaped the notice of many companies whose products—single-serving dinners, for example—are aimed at the single market.

The singles portrayed in commercials for these products seem carefree and happy, usually surrounded by numerous friends of both sexes. Yet a great many single people are lonely, and their biggest complaint is the difficulty they have meeting other single people who share their interests.

Against this backdrop, it is no surprise that video dating services have met with such success. Today's professional man or woman keeps a busy work schedule but also expects to have an active social life. Video dating addresses the social needs of this burgeoning, elite group by providing a unique, effective way for single people to meet without cruising bars.

Here is the way these video dating services work: The client pays to have himself or herself interviewed on videotape. What is the client looking for in a relationship? Does this client enjoy his or her job? Does he or she want a family?

That tape may then be viewed by other "club" members. At the same time, the new member is permitted to view tapes and select several people to meet. When a man and woman express a desire to meet each other, names are exchanged. The members are then on their own to arrange a rendezvous.

David Gresty, founder and owner of Getting Together in Ft. Lauderdale, Florida, believes that video eliminates the difficult aspects of meeting that new person. "The dynamics of video make the thing work," he said. "During the interview, the person is in motion, talking, articulating, expressing thoughts and emotions. It gives the person watching the tape a chance to be attracted in a multidimensional way."

Running a video dating service has special attraction for the person just starting out in video. The video skills needed are minimal. Most of these services use one stationary camera. The client relaxes in a comfortable chair on which the camera has been focused. The person operating the camera also does the interviewing, asking his or her own questions or those that have been selected beforehand by the client.

Many entrepreneurs running video dating services enjoy the work because it allows such close contact with people. You are a matchmaker. "This Saturday I'm going to our tenth wedding," said Dottie Nelson, who operates a video dating service in Louisville, Kentucky. What could be more satisfying?

If you think that running a video dating service is for you, there are several things to consider. One, your geographical location. There already are several very successful video dating services operating in New York City, for example. So unless you are well capitalized and are set for a fierce competitive struggle, the Big Apple will not be for you. At the same time, if you are located in a very small town, you may have trouble rounding up enough members to make a video dating service interesting. The best location would be a medium-sized city that has not yet been introduced to video dating, but has a large professional single population that would be receptive to the idea.

Several of the larger video dating services have begun franchising. This may be an attractive alternative. For an investment of several thousand dollars, you will have the support of an operation that is already successful. In most cases, the franchising arrangement will give you all the information and help you will need to set up your business, advertise it, and run it well.

If you would rather remain independent, but would like the detailed advice of someone in the business, Joan Hendrickson, owner of the Georgetown Connection in Washington, D.C., serves as a consultant and will give you all the information you need in a one-day session. (Dottie Nelson is one of Joan's protégées.) Joan charges a one-day fee for her service, and for that price you get the benefit of her experience and can profit from some of her mistakes. "I was not making any money for a long time," admitted Joan. "But now the people I train make money very quickly."

If you are looking for a video career where you can be the silent observer behind a camera, recording events but never taking part in them, video dating is not for you. Unless you plan to hire someone to interview clients, you will have to interact with each customer yourself. You must impress the potential customer who walks in the front door. Also, you must capture the best qualities of each client on videotape. That means developing an appropriate interviewing style. You want your client to relax, and he can only do that if he senses that you are comfortable in your role as interviewer.

During the interviewing for this book, I met a video expert who was unsuccessful at running a video dating service. It was obvious why he failed. His manner was aggressive and businesslike, well suited to many other video careers, but not one in video dating. He was hardly the type who would help to relax a first-time visitor to a video dating service.

In fact, most of the entrepreneurs involved in video dating not only sympathize but empathize with their clients. They have a genuine interest in single people because they experienced firsthand the plight of the single professional. "I got divorced when I was thirty-seven after being married for sixteen years," said Joe O'Connell, who began People Resources in New York in 1982. "I moved into the city and knew no one. The bar scene was not my cup of tea."

Joe had been a school principal in Bethpage, Long Island, and was looking for a new career where he could use his talents as a trained counselor. He decided that combining video with a dating service would be a perfect match. He was right. When he left People Resources in 1983, it had 1,700 members and was still growing.

Running People Resources dramatically changed Joe's life. "I went from the very dull existence of a high school principal to being sought after as a leading authority on singles lifestyles," he said. "I've been on ten different TV shows and I've been written up in every major magazine."

Joe, an entrepreneur to the core, said he enjoyed creating People Resources. But once it was up and running successfully, he felt the urge to begin something new. He sold People Resources and now is vice-president for Winner Communications, where he once again is involved in start-up projects and also gets to use the marketing and advertising expertise he developed running People Resources.

Caroline Yorke, who bought People Resources with a partner, is also single and came to the video dating service as a client. Caroline was so impressed with People Resources and the potential of video dating—not only as a businesswoman but as a single person using the service—that she traveled around the country, visiting competitors. She was convinced video dating was the job for her. "Video dating is here to stay," she predicted.

David Gresty, owner of Ft. Lauderdale's Getting Together, is a scientist who also studied philosophy. David was divorced in 1978. "If you are a new single, someone who has been married and divorced, I think you understand that there are a lot of problems in becoming single again," he reflected.

Joan Hendrickson was another who could relate to the problems of suddenly being single. Joan had been married for twenty-three years and raised three daughters when she went through a painful separation and divorce. Perhaps you, too, can relate to the dilemma of being single, but can't imagine starting a new business based on such a small fact. Of course, running a video dating service also was the farthest thing from Joan's mind. It just so happened that she was entering the job market possessing few skills with which to impress prospective employers. The only job she could land was as an interviewer in a new video dating service that had been set up by two men in Washington, D.C. Joan discovered she had a real talent for drawing people out and capturing their personalities on tape. She also enjoyed the role of matchmaker. When the two men went bankrupt, Joan scraped together her life savings to buy the business.

Of course, not everyone running a video dating service is single. Beth Cohen, who established Rittenhouse Contacts in Philadelphia after consulting with Joan, is married with two children. Beth has many single friends and became concerned that so many of them were having difficulty meeting people. A lawyer, she left her job with a large, prestigious Philadelphia firm, and now runs Rittenhouse Contacts and practices law part time at a smaller firm.

Dottie Nelson, who also is married with children, was equally dismayed by the singles scene in Louisville. A former seamstress and free-lance artist, Dottie is astounded by her own success. "If you had told me I would be running a video dating service, I would have laughed in your face," she said.

Once you've decided that video dating is for you, the next decision you will face is where to set up shop. Your impulse might be to scrimp on location in order to save money. Don't do it. In video dating, as in real estate, there are three factors that count: location, location, and location.

All of the video dating people I interviewed felt it was crucial to have a prestigious location to impress potential clients. Because most of these services hope to attract professional, affluent individuals, a tastefully furnished office in a convenient part of town was viewed as important.

People Resources location at 57th Street and Fifth Avenue is a plus. One of the company's original financial backers was Bob Villency, president of Maurice Villency, a well-known New York furniture chain. As a result, the video dating service has offices that are attractively furnished with luxuriously upholstered wine-colored chairs, mirrored walls and coffee tables, thick beige carpeting, and lush green plants. Joe O'Connell estimates that the company spent $50,000 on its video equipment, but more than double that amount on its offices.

Offices for the Georgetown Connection are more modest but no less impressive. Joan Hendrickson has housed her service in a charming townhouse in Washington's picturesque Georgetown. The offices are furnished in a homey fashion, with many of Joan's own personal belongings scattered around. The effect is warm and friendly, the exact image that Joan is trying to project.

Several other video dating officials cited location and office decor as important elements in the success of the business. Beth Cohen's service, for example, is located on

Philadelphia's classy Rittenhouse Square. And Dottie Nelson didn't think twice about seeking out offices in Louisville's high-rent district.

All of these video dating entrepreneurs are conscious of the stigma many people attach to ordinary or computer dating services. Joe O'Connell, who checked out many of the dating services himself, felt some of the people were dishonest. "Many of them have bad reputations," he said. Added Joan: "There are people exploiting singles and it infuriates me."

An elegantly furnished office is one cosmetic touch that can help impress a client. But most of these services follow through in more substantive ways to ensure clients that the service is a credible one. In setting up the service, you should formulate a comprehensive application form that will give you all the information you will need to verify a client's claims.

People Resources makes it routine to check out everyone who signs on. Rather than resenting such intrusion, most clients welcome it. That way they are guaranteed that anyone they will be meeting actually is what the profile says. To verify every member, People Resources takes several forms of identification, photos, and has each client fill out an extensive contract.

Joan Hendrickson also insists on several forms of identification and additional information on employment. "I have a lot of information on the application, so if I'm suspicious I check the person out," she said. "I encourage younger women to meet their dates in a public place for the first time." Of course, because Joan runs a very personalized agency, she gets to know most of her clients. "I know all of my guys," she said. "We have never had any trouble."

Introlens, which began in White Plains, New York, and now has offices in New Jersey, Manhattan, Long Island, and

Philadelphia, requires clients to fill out a detailed six-page questionnaire. "We keep abreast of all our clients and deal with everyone one to one," said Maureen White, vice-president.

Of course, even though you have in your possession extensive information on each client, this data should not be handed out indiscriminately to other clients. In addition to the detailed contract, you should have each client fill out a short questionnaire that can be shown to other clients.

This shorter questionnaire should only have the client's first name, no home address, and no phone number. The client should state an occupation, but not a company or firm. Remember, you are promising each client that he or she will meet only those clients he or she has selected. To prevent other clients from contacting these people, you must guard their identities. Names should be exchanged only when both parties agree they want to meet.

The questions on the short questionnaire should include other information that would be of interest to a possible date. While religion may be a taboo question on some applications, it is a necessity here. After all, why waste someone's time if he is determined to date only those of his own religion?

Other questions should bring out the client's personality. What are the person's hobbies? Favorite foods? Best qualities? Faults? Musical interests? Does he smoke? Does she like dogs? What is his image of the perfect date? What is her idea of the perfect vacation? You want to ask the right questions to elicit the best answers. Don't be afraid to inject some of yourself into it. What questions would you like to have answered if you were searching for someone?

Most of the video dating services require clients to sign a waiver acknowledging that the video service is making no claims about the results. You should do the same. Even so, as

Maureen said, "You can't please everyone." Joan Hendrickson was hauled into small claims court by a client upset that he didn't find the perfect match. Because of the signed agreement, Joan won, but she feels badly that even one client had to go away feeling he was cheated.

While an impressive office is important for these video dating services, a good client list also is crucial. It is impossible to run a good video dating service without enough well-qualified clients to make it interesting.

Keeping a healthy client list is an unending process. If you are successful at what you do, you have to expect some of your members will no longer need your services. Therefore, you must constantly be replenishing your supply.

The first step, of course, is to round up enough members to begin your service. There are many ways to accomplish this task. At People Resources, for example, each staff member was given the assignment to bring in twenty people. In addition, People Resources ran a special introductory offer for $100. "We didn't open our doors until we had two hundred members," Joe O'Connell recalled. It took two months to sign up that many people. What was the response of people invited to join? "Laughter, reluctance, intrigue, adventure," recalled Joe. "It sounded like a good bargain at a hundred dollars."

Dottie Nelson used similar tactics in order to get her service in Louisville off the ground. She took in seventy-five free members. Today, she has more than one hundred paying members.

Don't be reluctant to call on single friends and relatives to join. And encourage them to talk up the service to their friends and relatives.

Take out an advertisement in the local paper announcing your service. Be sure to include a telephone number. Be there to answer the phone, or hire someone to answer calls for you. In the beginning, don't rely on an answering service. Many people calling to inquire about the service are just looking for an excuse to hang up. Don't give them one.

Whoever answers these first few calls should be ready to provide satisfactory answers to the caller's questions and dismiss any fears about video dating. Don't make the service sound mysterious. Nothing will turn off a potential client more than holding out information with the promise that "If you'll just visit our office we'll be able to give you more details." That approach smacks of high pressure. The implication is that if you can get this guy in the door, you can sign him up. Tell him everything he wants to know before he visits so that he will know exactly what to expect.

Consider offering free demonstrations to your first few customers. Even if you only have a few videotapes to show, it will give the customer an idea of what the service is about. A client viewing tapes for the first time at any one of the video dating services cannot help but be impressed. The men and women come across as being intelligent and articulate. Any idea that a video dating service attracts misfits or losers is immediately dispelled. "Video brings in a higher class of people," said Joan.

Once a video dating service has a core client list, it can begin to add others and should begin thinking about how to accomplish that feat. A great deal of the business is built through word of mouth—one satisfied friend telling another one. Yet Joe O'Connell estimated that when he ran People Resources only 25 percent of his business was word of mouth. "It's not spread throughout town as quickly as a good steakhouse," he said. "You tell only your best friends. You might tell your business clients about it, but not that you belong."

As a result, Joe and others believe that advertising is important. Two months after launching People Resources, Joe took out a full-page ad in *The New York Times*. While the cost is high, Joe believes it's worth every penny. *"The New York Times* proved to be a major source of new members for us," he said. Joe pointed out that the *Times* lends credibility to People Resources. "People who read an ad like that are going to say, 'These guys are serious. This is a professional operation.'" Caroline Yorke said that People Resources is continuing to advertise in the *Times*.

David Gresty said that advertising and public relations expenditures account for a great part of the cost of operating Getting Together. The service has run ads on TV and radio, as well as in magazines and newspapers. David also is a firm believer in direct mail because it is possible to target the audience he wants to reach by purchasing the appropriate list.

Luckily, video dating appears to have captured the fancy of the media. Nearly every video dating service has been the subject of articles in major magazines as well as segments on TV shows. "The video is a new way of doing something, but also there are tons of singles and a lot of interest in their activities," said Beth Cohen. Within months of the opening of Rittenhouse Contacts, the *Philadelphia Inquirer* did a major feature on the service, which ran on the front page of its family section. After that, Beth discussed her new business on "AM Philadelphia" and three other TV shows.

People Resources was the subject of a full hour on "The David Susskind Show." Joe O'Connell appeared on ten TV shows. Other articles on People Resources have appeared in *Glamour*, *Mademoiselle*, the *New York Daily News*, and *TV Guide*.

While some of these opportunities for media exposure seem to fall into one's lap, others are hard fought for. Joan Hendrickson sent a steady stream of letters to "The Phil Donahue Show." "I told stories about what went on at the

Connection—a little love story, a little sappy story," she recalled. After numerous rejection letters, she finally received a call from the show's producer. Joan appeared on "The Phil Donahue Show" in 1979. "I figured if I could get on 'Phil Donahue,' I could do anything," she said. "So I wrote to the *Wall Street Journal*. It took me a year and a half, but I got a front page story." In addition, Joan has been a guest twice on Larry King's all-night talk show on the Mutual Broadcasting System where guests can call in and ask questions.

If anyone wonders whether all the aggravation is worth it, ask Joan. "I wasn't making any money until after 'Donahue,'" she said. After each major media event, Joan reports, there is an upturn in business. "After the *Wall Street Journal* story I did a lot of consulting work," she said. "That was a very good year. The *Journal* gave me a lot of credibility." Following an appearance on Washington's "PM Magazine" TV show, Georgetown Connection signed up fifteen new members within thirty days.

Once all these new members come piling through the door, what does the service do with them?

On the initial visit, all these services work hard to put the prospective client at ease. There is little pressure to force a customer to sign on the dotted line. Because most of the clients are professional people, such hard sell would be annoying.

Most clients are nervous during their first visit. Many are unsure what to expect from a dating service. Then there is the fear of being videotaped. Consequently, some services reserve the first visit for getting acquainted with the video dating service employees (including the person who will do the interviewing during the taping), filling out the application, and viewing tapes of other clients.

Some general guidelines: Make a point of greeting each new client no matter how busy you are. Especially in the beginning when you are building a reputation, it will make each client feel important. Don't let a potential customer sit in the waiting room. Professional people are busy, too, and will resent waiting until 2:30 P.M. for a 2:00 P.M. appointment. Be sure to schedule enough time with each client so that your appointments do not run together.

Have refreshments available. Coffee, tea, soda, and wine are the best beverages to have on hand. It isn't necessary to have food. Especially if you are going to be videotaping, you don't want your subject munching on potato chips.

Once you have met the client and have offered him something to drink, don't plunge right into talking about the business. Instead, try to find out something about him. Most people are comfortable when discussing themselves, and it also will serve as a warm-up for what he will say on videotape.

Joan Hendrickson's technique is impressive. Her approach is a go-slow one, aimed at relaxing the client until he is comfortable with the idea of being videotaped.

With few exceptions, Joan answers her own phone. "I tell them all they want to know on the phone, what we do, how it works, the price," she explained. "Then they come in and I offer them a demonstration." Joan encourages prospective clients to view other people's applications, just to assure them of the caliber of the people who come to the Georgetown Connection. They can choose tapes they want to see. If they decide to join, Joan gives them several profiles of others to take home and study.

On the second visit, Joan will videotape her client, so she always advises them to wear something colorful. "When they come back, they are more comfortable about doing it because they know the place, they know us," she said.

Joan first offers the client wine or coffee. She will chat as long as necessary to make sure the client is relaxed. Joan has become adept at reading body language. For example, if she notices very rapid eye movement, tightly clenched fists, or arms crossed on the chest, she knows the client is still anxious. "I flip on the set only when I feel they're comfortable," she said.

Joan records only two to three minutes because she has discovered that is plenty of time for a client to make up his mind on a prospective date. (Caroline Yorke reported that People Resources also has reduced the length of its tapes from five minutes to three minutes. "Five minutes is much too long," said Caroline.)

After the videotape is made, Joan allows the client to watch it. During the entire process, Joan is not just a passive participant. By questioning the client and directing the interview, she attempts to get the best of that client on tape. "The video is a very effective tool," she said. "The personality actually comes out on the tape." She laughed over one fact. "I sometimes try to keep men's egos down so the women won't be turned off. But the ego comes charging through. It's uncanny."

Not only does Joan want to capture the essence of each client's personality on videotape, she wants them to have a good time while she is accomplishing that. After all, dating is a social event and should be fun. "It's important for them to feel good when they leave here, and they do, because of all the attention that is focused on them," said Joan.

At People Resources, Caroline said the concept of the videotape was altered slightly. Instead of merely answering questions, the client chats with the interviewer. "The new format seems to have been successful," said Caroline. "People who have not been chosen before now are being chosen."

At Getting Together, David Gresty said the interviewer spends about thirty minutes preparing people for the video tape. "Within ten or twenty seconds, people forget they're being interviewed and it becomes a natural conversation," David said.

Some video dating services guarantee each client a certain number of dates. Others, however, make no such promises. Joan Hendrickson has, on occasion, had to tell a client that not one of the people selected is available for a date. "It's very hard," she confessed. "But you soften it by saying things like this person is going back to an ex-spouse or moving away."

The officials who operate video dating services are so enthusiastic about the concept, it's almost as if they wonder how men and women met before the video revolution.

Once a video entrepreneur is successfully running a video dating service, what next? Should the service be expanded or maintained at its present size? The answer varies depending upon the individual.

Michael Sacco, owner of Introlens, is one who would like to expand, not only domestically but internationally. The company has been an aggressive competitor seeking to sell franchises in other locales.

Even though Joan has been successful, she intends to keep Georgetown Connection small. She plans to continue her consulting role, but she does not want to franchise. After she was on "Phil Donahue," she opened another office in McLean, Virginia. She soon discovered, however, that she had stretched herself too thin and was losing contact with her clients. "I had to get back to basics," she said, explaining why she closed the McLean office. "I tried doing parties and seminars, but what I'm here for is to do the matching. It's what I do best."

Of course, worrying about whether to remain small and successful or go international may seem like a remote problem to someone just getting started in video dating. But the success of existing video dating services can work to your benefit. Because these services are becoming well known, there is less apprehension over video dating. That fact can help you gain acceptance for it in your own city.

You might even take advantage of the success of these services by joining with them. Definitely investigate owning a franchise. At least two services, Introlens in New York and Getting Together in Ft. Lauderdale, are interested in finding qualified people to operate franchises in cities around the United States. Be warned, however, that you will have to demonstrate that you possess the business acumen and financial resources to run one of these franchises successfully.

Even if you decide that franchising is not for you, visiting these successful services and learning all you can about the business can increase your own knowledge of video dating. That's what Caroline Yorke did before she bought People Resources. She approached some services by phone, others in person. Sometimes Caroline presented herself as a client, other times as a journalist gathering information on video dating. With some, she was candid and said she was thinking of starting a video dating service.

Caroline encountered no hostility on the part of the video dating companies, even when she said she was a possible competitor. The entire experience answered a lot of questions for her before she involved herself in actually running a video dating business. She was able to assess not only how each service handled phone inquiries but also how they dealt with clients who visited the offices.

If you reject franchising but would like to obtain more information, you might consider spending a day with Joan Hendrickson.

The investment for a video dating service can vary greatly. Joan Hendrickson began her service with an investment of about $5,000, while Joe O'Connell estimates that he and his partners spent more than $100,000, in large part because of their location near Fifth Avenue. Your investment could be nearer to Joan's if you began your service by purchasing consumer video equipment. But you must budget for rent, and this could be a major expense since you want a good location. Also budget for maintaining your facilities, telephone bills, advertising costs, office supplies, and refreshments.

You now possess enough information to launch your own video dating service. What you must decide is whether it is suited to your personality. Video dating is attractive to the novice because it requires minimal technical skills. But that fact may be discouraging to you later on if you want to become more creative. Also, the demands of constantly meeting the public and appearing upbeat may prove tiring.

For those working in video dating, however, the experience has proved to be exhilarating. The rewards—both monetary and psychological—are ample. All involved believe that video dating will increase in popularity in the future, and they see their companies well positioned to profit. Perhaps yours will be, too.

12

Video for a Consumer Market

ONE OF the most promising areas for the video entrepreneur is the consumer market. Video has taken over where home movies left off. Whether the event is a wedding, bar mitzvah, backyard barbecue, or birthday party, the consumer is looking to preserve such moments on videotape.

Even though many consumers now own their own video cameras, it is often inconvenient for them to tape their own events. After all, Uncle Harry and Aunt Jo expect to have a good time at their niece's wedding, and will not be too thrilled about spending most of the party behind a camera. Then again, even the best video hobbyist is apt to be an amateur and his videotape of the event will show that (especially if he has had one too many glasses of champagne). A consumer who hires a video professional does so because he wants to enjoy his own party and have the event recorded skillfully. He needs your service.

The consumer market is probably the easiest one for you to crack. For one thing, you can do it in your spare time on weekends, when many of these social events are likely to occur. That means you can work your regular job while testing the video field. If you decide it is a good career for you and you find your services are in such demand that you can make a good enough profit to support yourself, then you can quit your job and jump in full time. If it is not to your liking, however, you will not have lost anything and, in fact, will have picked up some additional income and made a few new friends. Another plus for the consumer market is that it exists everywhere. A couple in Toledo, Ohio, is just as apt to want a wedding videotaped as a couple in Los Angeles. And it is a market where word of mouth can really bring in a lot of business. One satisfied customer tells a friend how pleased he was with your service and before you know it, you are videotaping that friend's anniversary party.

Of course, there are thorns along with the roses. Many consumers have been conditioned by television and will expect the videotape of their backyard barbecue to resemble a get-together at Southfork. You have to be sure to scale down their expectations, unless they really are willing to pay for three or four cameras, lots of special effects, and hours of editing (and unless you are skilled enough to produce such extras). Assure them that you will do a good, professional job within the budget that you are given.

If you decide to aim for the consumer market, start slowly. To minimize your investment, rent some video equipment from a local video shop. A good first step would be to practice videotaping a big party before you start to line up clients and charge for your service. Offer to videotape a friend's party free of charge. Warn him that this is a practice run and may or may not produce a good videotape. Approach this job as you would one where you are being paid. Take careful notes along the way so that you will have a record of everything you did and when you did it. Be particularly aware of any problems you encountered. After the job is over, you can sit down and figure out what went wrong or right and how you would approach the taping differently next time.

Anyone who is going to come to you for your service will

want to see some samples of your work. You might have to continue to videotape for free until you have several tapes you are proud to show. Once you have reached that point, you are ready to advertise and charge people for your service.

Another plus with the consumer market is that there are many opportunities for you to advertise your service. As discussed in chapter 4, many of these advertising outlets are surprisingly low cost.

One of the best places to be seen is in the Yellow Pages. You might want to consider listing yourself under two headings, Video as well as Wedding Services and Supplies. Make your ad simple and direct. Be sure to invest in an answering machine so that potential customers can leave a message. (Even though this seems like an obvious thing to do, and relatively inexpensive since answering machines have come down greatly in price, I was amazed to discover, while writing this book, how many video people have overlooked this important detail.)

You will also want to investigate running ads in local newspapers. While you might not have enough cash to run a full-page ad in *The New York Times*, there are many smaller newspapers whose ad rates would be more in keeping with your budget. Don't overlook supermarket shoppers, local TV magazines, or community newsletters. Many churches now take advertisements in their Sunday bulletins. The price is very reasonable, and what better place to contact people who are thinking about weddings?

With a little legwork, you can manage to contact engaged couples directly. Make it routine to go through the engagement announcements in your local paper. Then, using your phone book, attach an address to the name. Print or type up a brochure that details your services and gives prices. It is a good idea to enclose a cover letter to make the mailing more personal.

After a decent interval has gone by, you may want to follow up the mailings with phone calls. Be warned that many people can be turned off by phone solicitations and you may have people hang up in your ear. If you keep your sales pitch low-key and friendly, you are likely to get better results.

Another way of drumming up business is to establish a relationship with a still photographer in your community. Even with the appeal of video, most couples also want still photographs. After all, you can't prop up a videocassette on your piano.

Some people who answer your advertisements may be unsure whether they really want a videotape of their special event. You must sell them on the idea. Actually, that should be an easy task, because there are dozens of reasons why a video record is so attractive. Here is an endorsement of the videotaped wedding from one video expert:

"The tape will last a lifetime, so even if you don't have a machine right now, the tape will be good five, ten, or fifteen years from now to show your children or grandchildren," said Fred Russo, a videographer in Connecticut. "Month by month, year by year, more people are finding out about the video wedding. As consumers become more exposed to it, and as more machines are sold, it will continue to grow."

Some potential customers may be afraid that you will intrude on the dignity of the event. In fact, a video camera is less intrusive than a still camera. When the video camera is running, there is no noise. You or one of your assistants can move around, quietly recording without making your presence felt. Then too, most video cameras operate with available light, so there is no need to set up bright, hot lights or annoy people with a flash.

John Phillips of Video Replay in Connecticut said he can shoot with available light in most churches, except those with very dark stained-glass windows. "If we do have to augment the lighting, we bounce the light off the ceiling," he explained. You should avoid hitting people in the face with harsh lights.

Once you have assured your customers that their event will not be turned into a presidential news conference, you can begin to sell them on video's other benefits. Some of these benefits are obvious. No still photograph can compete with a moving, talking record of the event. If you are recording a wedding ceremony, for example, you capture the entire atmosphere. You can hear the wedding march, Aunt Tilly sniffling, the bride and groom exchanging vows. Perhaps the only thing you can't do is preserve the smell of the flowers. But you will be able to see the flowers and everything else in the church, because with a video camera you can slowly pan the room to give the viewer an idea of what the church really looked like that day.

There are many good still photographers, but let's face it, most of them cover weddings like robots. They have a certain number of standard pictures to take (bride walks down aisle, father kisses bride goodbye, bride throws bouquet) and they snap them. There is very little spontaneity.

With video, there will be many candid moments. And because the completed videotape can run more than an hour, everyone can get into the act.

Inevitably there will be guests who miss a wedding because of a prior commitment. With a videotape of the wedding, these absent guests will feel as if they've been there. And because copies can be made, the happy couple can even send extras to out-of-town relatives.

To do a top-notch job of recording a wedding, bar mitzvah, or other event, you must plan ahead.

You must have a discussion with the principals to find out exactly what they expect. If it's a wedding, do they want your taping to begin at the church or at the bride's home? If it's a party, should you record the arrival of each guest, or limit your taping to when the party is in full swing?

You will want to get an idea of which people you should photograph most. At a wedding, should you follow the bride and groom around? How much footage should be devoted to the parents and how much to friends? If there are special people the host wants to include, make sure these people are pointed out to you. Otherwise, they are apt to get lost in the crowd shots.

It is imperative that you visit each and every place where you will be taping. "You have to go out and do a site inspection; that's a must," said Haven McKinney, a videographer in Washington, D.C. "Murphy's Law will zap you every time."

You will need to know what physical restrictions you might run into at the church, synagogue, reception hall, or restaurant. Will there be enough available light? (Often there is, but some churches can be very dimly lit and could pose problems you should deal with beforehand.) The best time to do this inspection is during the rehearsal in the case of a wedding or bar or bas mitzvah. For a party, you should arrange a special time with the host.

Ask about any special rules that the church or synagogue may have with respect to cameras and light. In some synagogues, for example, a bar mitzvah ceremony must be shot with available light from the rear of the synagogue, thus creating a special challenge for the videographer. Haven noted that this also presents certain problems for recording the audio portion of the event. If you operate with one mike from the rear of the church, it will be easy to pick up the cantor, who most likely will have a strong booming voice, but nearly impossible to hear the young boy or girl. "You have to mike everybody separately," said Haven.

Even if the church doesn't restrict you from videotaping

at the altar, the priest or minister may object. Make sure that the bride and groom have discussed the matter with the officiating clergy. You don't want to be surprised the morning of the wedding and have no plan to fall back on.

It is also imperative to do an equipment check far enough in advance so that you can get replacements if needed.

While it is possible to cover an event by yourself, most videographers have hired assistants. Having a second person on the scene means that you can better handle any crisis that occurs. Especially during a lively party, that second person can be visualizing the next shot while you are concentrating on the current one. Most videographers, to keep the cost down, only use one camera. But if your client is willing to pay for it, you and your assistant can each run a camera and then edit together the best footage.

If you are hired to cover a wedding and reception, it is not unusual to end up with six hours of videotape. Obviously, you cannot just turn over so much raw videotape to the bride and groom. You must edit it down, cut out some of the superfluous scenes, put the various events into some sort of sequence that the viewer can follow, and make the whole thing exciting and fun to watch.

If you do not have your own editing facility, then you can probably arrange to rent a facility or machine for each job. Once you build up your business, however, editing equipment will be a must. In the consumer area, everything should be edited. "The tape needs to be cleaned up," agrees John Phillips. "I don't think I've done one so far where I haven't done something stupid like leaving the camera running for five seconds and getting a picture of somebody's foot. That sort of thing needs to be taken out."

John also reports that some of the glitches can be beyond your control. During the videotaping of one wedding, for example, the priest discovered he had forgotten the wine chalice. He left the bridal party standing on the altar for fifteen minutes while he went to search for it. John's camera continued to roll, but he later edited those fifteen minutes out.

Albert Dabah, owner of Video Portfolios in New York, believes it's good business to create the best-looking tape possible. "It helps the business a lot when we can make the tape look good," he said. "You want the party to move quickly. Of course we allow the clients to come in and give us their ideas because what may be boring to us may not be to them. For example, people want to see their family dancing at weddings."

Albert also adds his own special touches, which help to distinguish his service from others. At the beginning, he will show close-ups of the couple's wedding invitation, with music chosen by the couple playing in the background. He also includes titles ("The Wedding of John and Mary," for example). At the end, he wraps up the tape with a fast-paced look back at the wedding and reception. These little vignettes, as Albert calls them, have proven to be very popular with his customers.

Every now and then, it will happen. You will be asked to videotape a wedding or party that is so dull you have a hard time staying awake. You need a real miracle to make such a get-together look exciting. But with the magic of video, you can do it. With some editing, you can make the party take on a faster pace. Cut out those glum faces and pause more on the smiling ones. And if the music sounded like a dirge, throw out the audio and add some zippy music of your own.

Even though you may be eager for the business when you are getting started, be careful that you do not promise your client more than you can deliver. If you have not mastered fancy editing techniques, don't promise him any. Show him your sample videotapes. If he wants something over and beyond what you can deliver, tell him so. It is better to turn down the job than wind up with a dissatisfied customer who may hurt your business if he tells others.

If you have already priced your service reasonably, don't start to drop your price so drastically that you will have a hard time making a profit. Even though you are trying to build a client base, you will be unhappy if you feel you are giving your work away. Whether you charge by the job or the hour, you should have a price that reflects the time and effort you put into it. That also means compensation for the cost of the equipment and the services of any assistants you may hire.

Don't be vague about the price with the client. A good idea is to have a price list printed up so that there won't be any misunderstandings. Here is a sample of what your handout explaining the cost for videotaping a wedding could look like:

ATLAS VIDEO

200 MAIN STREET

HOMETOWN, U.S.A.

Plan A
    Involves videotaping of the entire event—bride's home, ceremony, and reception. Cost: $800.

Plan B
    Involves four hours of videotaping beginning with the ceremony and into the reception. Cost: $650.

Plan C
    Involves taping ceremony only. Cost: $400.

Videotapes can be on VHS, Betamax, or 3/4-inch format.
All videotapes are in color with sound and music.
Editing costs are included. Additional tapes $100 each.

Besides videotaping actual events like weddings and parties, with videotape you can create events. One idea that is catching on is the video family album. This is almost a minidocumentary on a family showing each family member relaxing at home, enjoying his hobbies, and interacting with others. This family album could be shot on a special day—Thanksgiving, Christmas, someone's birthday—or during an ordinary day.

Such a videotape can challenge your creativity as you consider how best to present the many facets of each member's personality. A great deal will be expressed merely by the background you choose to photograph these people in front of. You can show the introspective side of a person by videotaping him at work in his den. Or the outgoing side as he leads a family basketball game. You can display the warmth of the family by capturing them around the dinner table as they share talk of the day's activities.

A family could find many uses for this videotape. It will be around for a long time for succeeding generations to enjoy. Also, it could be sent to relatives who visit infrequently but would still like to spend some time with their family.

Along those same lines, you should also think about selling the video telegram. This is a videotape with a message that can be sent to a faraway relative or friend. The message can be as broad as one expressed in a family album ("We're all fine and wish you were here") or specific (Happy Birthday, Anniversary, etc.).

The videogram can be approached in many different ways. It can be a personal message to the celebrant from the person who commissioned the videotape. Or, you can offer to include other extras. If it's a birthday message for Diane, how about shots of celebrities who share Diane's birthday?

Depending on how elaborate you wanted to get, you could even include someone reading a horoscope prediction for Diane. Perhaps you have videotaped an entertainer who would be willing to appear on the tape as a fortune teller. Or, you might have an entertainer who would agree to sing "Happy Birthday." (This, once again, might be a good time for bartering, offering the entertainer a free videotape of a recent performance in exchange for his services.)

There are other video services that can be offered to the consumer.

At present, many consumers keep a visual record of valuables by photographing such items and attaching a printed description of each item and its worth. Needless to say, this can be a time-consuming chore. Also, some still photographs cannot properly convey the appearance of, say, Oriental rugs or precious antiques.

Videotape can. Rather than photograph each item individually, you can pan an entire room. Because videotape also has sound, the owner can even walk around the room, pointing to certain objects for emphasis, describing them, and stating their value. Once the tape has been made, it can be placed in the consumer's safe-deposit vault for safekeeping.

Those who are working in the insurance area point out there are clear advantages for video that can be emphasized when selling the service to the consumer. "When you get home insurance, the last thing the agent will tell you as he is walking out the door is, you'd better take pictures of your valuables," said Bill Hood, owner of Custom Video Productions in Clearwater, Florida. "But by the time you pay for the film, take the picture, and get it developed, you have the cost of what it takes to have it done in video." Bill said he charges $50 an hour for his service and usually can videotape an entire home in an hour.

This service can be marketed in two ways, directly to the consumer or through insurance agents. A newspaper ad would reach both of these markets. Another way to reach consumers might be through flyers placed on automobile windows in shopping areas. To reach the insurance agents, you might make up a list of local sales agents in your community by going through the Yellow Pages. These people could then be reached by a direct mail campaign or by phone. Remember, you are not necessarily trying to sell the service to the agents, but to convince them to recommend your service to their customers. The agents will be encouraged to do that once they are convinced that a video record could make their job easier when a customer is filing a claim. Be sure to play up that advantage of your service.

Remember one important fact when you create and sell services to consumers: Everyone is a consumer, including you. Recognizing this will help you think up new uses for video in this area. And it will help you to evaluate sales potential. If it isn't a service that you would be interested in buying yourself, then chances are no one else will be interested in it either.

The consumer area presents many challenges and opportunities to the video entrepreneur. It can prove to be a stepping stone to other areas of video. But many people discover it is so much to their liking that they stay and expand. With more consumers investing in videocassette recorders, it is easy to share the enthusiasm of these entrepreneurs. Videotape is on its way to becoming an important communications medium for the average American.

13

Mistakes
to Avoid

STUDIES SHOW that between one-quarter and one-third of all new businesses fail within the first year of operation, and video businesses are not excluded from this statistic. Video businesses are vulnerable because they are breaking new ground. The same factors that make video so exciting and interesting also mean that it may be more difficult to manage and sell.

Be fully aware going in that no business takes care of itself. Look around your own neighborhood. Chances are that the small merchants who are doing well are vigilant. They are constantly in their shops keeping careful track of their stocks, managing their employees, and visiting with customers.

A new business requires more care and feeding. Its success or failure depends in large part on you, the owner, operator, creator, and manager.

No one can anticipate every problem. With proper planning, however, you can be prepared to deal with most major crises that may occur. Don't expect to have things go without a hitch. Recognize that there will be days when nothing seems to go right. Your goal should be to learn by your mistakes so you won't make the same ones over and over again.

As a starter, review these most commonly made mistakes and be sure you do not repeat them. By the time your business is humming along, you may have ten other "mistakes to avoid" to add to this list.

"I'm an artist, not a businessman."

You may be a marvelous video artist. But don't hide behind your creativity. It isn't enough to turn out good videotapes. You must know something about managing your business.

Sure, it's possible to succeed without knowing something about revenues and profits. It's possible, but difficult. It may take you much longer to make back your investment if you have ignored the basic economic facts about running your business.

"I know my idea will sell. Who needs to do research?"

Never launch a new business without thoroughly researching your idea. This means identifying the market and establishing whether there is a need for the service. Solicit the advice and opinions of people who are potential customers. In addition, present your proposal to professionals who know something about video, marketing, or the area you plan to specialize in.

It may be difficult to hear criticism of your idea. (That is why many entrepreneurs bounce their ideas off close friends and relatives who they know won't be critical.) But ask yourself, do you really want to go through all the time, money, and effort necessary to launch a new business if a check with several experts could show you that your idea has serious flaws?

Test the water first.

Some entrepreneurs are too eager to jump into the video business full time, believing it's all or nothing at all. Nothing could be farther from the truth. If you are unsure of the potential of your idea, operate your business on a part-time basis. Consumer video in particular is a perfect weekend business.

Part-time work will allow you to continue working at your regular job so you do not jeopardize your financial well-being. If you find your business building at a healthy rate, then you can make a full-time commitment.

"I can run my business on a shoestring. Who needs capital?"

Time and again video entrepreneurs underestimate the amount of money they will need to launch their business. Keep in mind, there are expenses you will have to meet right away—rent, equipment, employees, electricity, advertising, transportation, postage. In addition, you will have to continue to cover these expenses for quite some time until your business makes more money than it costs you. Then you will be making a profit.

When you are figuring out the amount you will need, be sure to be generous in your estimates. It is better to overestimate your expenses than underestimate and be unable to face your creditors.

"Sure the rent on Park Avenue is high, but it's impressive."

Everyone dreams of running his business from a luxuriously furnished suite in an elegant building. But unless the video business you are setting up dictates a swank address (video dating and some consumer services are included in that group), try not to spend a disproportionate amount of your income on rent. That does not mean, of course, that you should move into a run-down building in a dangerous neighborhood. But be sensible. If you have few customers visiting your shop, then there is less need for an expensive office. When you are a success, you can move.

"Who needs to advertise? The people who count will find me."

Too many video people disregard advertising. Often it's the last item on the list, lopped off when funds run out. Advertising is a must and can help you build your business more quickly. During the interviewing for this book, many a video entrepreneur boasted that he or she had become successful without spending a dime on advertising. But on closer questioning, each revealed how long it took to reach that success. A little advertising might have sped up the process. And advertising does not have to be expensive. There are many low-cost opportunities, as outlined in chapter 4.

"Dan is my right-hand man. I never check up on him."

Once you are no longer a one-man band, you will find you are managing other people. Whether these people are freelancers or actual employees, a lot is riding on your managerial abilities. Video is a creative endeavor and people create better when they enjoy their work. It is up to you to make sure they do.

But always keep in mind that no one cares about your business as much as you do. You are the owner. It's your reputation that is on the line. There's nothing wrong with giving your employees a little freedom, but continue to maintain a watchful eye.

"It's a video rolling pin. I know we'll sell a million."

In video, as in sports and comedy, timing is everything. You may think up the best new use for video, but if people aren't ready for it, they won't buy it.

Make sure your idea isn't too far ahead of its time. If it is, no amount of advertising or sales promotion will change peoples' minds and make it a success.

"Sure I could shoot weddings, but I'm determined to have a video legal business."

It is essential that you remain flexible while you are setting up and operating your new business. Don't back yourself into a corner, swearing you'll never do such-and-such. It may take you a while to build your business in one particular area, so be open to new ideas.

"Sure my business has grown, but I can still operate it out of my bedroom."

It finally has happened: After months or years of sacrificing and hard work, your business has taken off. So what are you doing still running it out of a shoebox? Sooner or later, it is time to admit the truth: Your business must move onto the next plateau.

This step may not be as easy as you think. Many entrepreneurs cannot quite believe that they are successful. They are fearful that if they make that final jump and set up an actual office or hire employees or incorporate, everything will fall apart. Chances are, if you made it this far, you will do just fine.

14

Off and Running

EMBARKING ON any new adventure can be exhilarating, and launching your own business may very well be your greatest career experience. There is a new sense of freedom as you realize that you are calling the shots. There is a newfound satisfaction in the work that you turn out. There is the excitement in knowing that you actually can make it on your own.

A video business can be especially satisfying. Video calls for a combination of talents. The video entrepreneur must be creative. But he should also have a good business sense. And it won't hurt if he is good at handling people, whether those people are his workers or his clients. Someone who is running a successful video business, who has had to put to work the whole range of his talents, no doubt will feel that he can do just about anything.

Working in video also brings with it the special attraction of being in a field that is bursting with activity. Everywhere we turn we read about the video revolution and what it will mean for our careers and personal lives. We know that video is not just a flash in the pan. If anything, the trend will accelerate in the years ahead. Future generations may indeed find video indispensable.

Because these events seem to be happening so quickly, it is understandable that you may want to jump into the fray immediately. And there is something to be said for being the first on your block to develop and market a particular application for video. Remember, if your idea cannot be protected, getting there first is the best strategy.

But avoid making any hasty decisions. Launching a business without doing your homework will doom you to failure. You want to be first, but most of all you want to be there for a long time.

Before you leap, take stock of the resources you will need to succeed in video and make sure you have an ample supply of each.

First, you will need financial resources. Be generous when you estimate how much money you will need. You want to be able to ride out those early days when you seem always to be writing checks but never receiving any. Don't plan to go down to your last penny. No business is worth your ending up on Skid Row.

Second, you will need physical resources. Many video businesses prove that the old saying still is true: Success is 1 percent inspiration and 99 percent perspiration. You will have to work at your business to make it a success. In the beginning it means handling many of the menial tasks yourself, while still having enough energy left for those jobs that require your special skills.

Third, you will need emotional resources. While a new business can be thrilling, there will be times when the emotional scale will tip in the other direction. Especially in those beginning days, there will be anxieties, fears, self-doubts, and depressions. There is a major difference, however. You are not trapped in some corporate maze where you must solve problems created by others. When you run your own business, you are the boss. If something goes wrong, you have the authority to deal with it.

When you are totally convinced that you have a video idea that can be successfully marketed, then it is time for you to start your business. That could be the hardest step—actually going out and doing what you have been talking about for months. The possibility of failure looms over you, and you may begin having second thoughts.

Have some confidence in yourself. If you have done a thorough research job, the chances are good that you will make it.

You may think that it will never happen, but one day your business will be a success. Your next thought may very well be about expanding and you will begin to investigate various strategies for growth. You may want to obtain a loan to help move your company onto the next plane.

With a business that is in operation, the bank or lending institution will be impressed by certain facts. First and foremost, your character and business acumen will be critically examined. It is crucial that you present books and records that are up to date and in good condition.

The bank will study your accounts receivable—that is, the amount of money that is owed to you by your customers. Obviously, it will hurt your case if you seem to be having trouble getting people to pay you. The bank also will study what you owe other people, including payments to free-lancers, fees if you have leased equipment, rent, utilities, and any other items.

Even before you approach a bank, you should know what kind of loan you are looking for. Basically, there are three types of money: short term, term borrowing, and equity capital. A short-term loan usually is obtained with a specific purpose in mind. In the case of a video business, you might want a short-term loan to buy additional equipment needed for a certain job. When the job is completed and you have been paid, you would pay off the loan. Term borrowing is money that you plan to pay back over a longer period of time, perhaps over more than five years.

Equity capital differs from a loan. You don't repay equity money. You receive the money in return for selling a part interest in your business. Anyone who buys equity in your company would share in the ownership. It probably will be quite some time before your company grows to the point where someone would be interested in investing in it. When that point is reached, you will have to make a decision on how you feel about relinquishing some control in order to see your company grow.

There are firms that supply venture capital to embryonic businesses that appear promising. Directories listing these venture-capital companies can be obtained through one of the large brokerage houses in New York.

If you are seeking venture capital, Tony Hoffman of Cralin & Co. advises not to wait until the last minute. "Unfortunately, most entrepreneurs seeking venture capital want the money yesterday," Tony said. Yet it usually takes a venture-capital firm several months to evaluate the company and then structure a deal. "Some entrepreneurs get themselves into a position where they'll do anything," Tony noted. Most of the investors who come to Cralin & Co. looking for companies to invest in do not want a controlling interest. In fact, Tony is inclined to be suspicious of an entrepreneur who appears too eager to sign away his entire company to an investor.

Running your own business can be a rewarding experience. But it is also hard work, especially during the crucial start-up period. There will be many details that will demand your attention. Keep in mind how important these first days will be to the success of your business. Many of the decisions that you make will determine whether your business makes it. In light of that fact, take the time to set up your business properly. Avoid making hasty decisions. Consider all the options. And once you have laid the foundation, continue to build on it.

Index